Sarah Oliver is a journalist and the author of numerous popular-culture titles, including *One Direction A to Z* and *Robert Pattinson A to Z*. She lives in Cheshire with her husband and in her spare time she sings in a worship band at her local church.

POLLYANNE

One Little Donkey's Amazing
Journey from the Knacker's Yard
to the West End Stage

Sarah Oliver

sphere

SPHERE

First published in Great Britain in 2012 by Sphere
Reprinted 2012 (twice)

A CIP catalogue record for this book
is available from the British Library.

ISBN 978-0-34900-098-5

Typeset in Palatino by M Rules
Printed and bound in Great Britain by
Clays Ltd, St Ives plc

Papers used by Sphere are from well-managed forests
and other responsible sources.

MIX
Paper from
responsible sources
FSC® C104740

Sphere
An imprint of
Little, Brown Book Group
100 Victoria Embankment
London EC4Y 0DY

An Hachette UK Company
www.hachette.co.uk

www.littlebrown.co.uk

Contents

Introduction by Sarah Oliver

John McLaren is a remarkable man, a true unsung hero. More than twenty years ago years ago, he founded Island Farm Donkey Sanctuary in the tiny village of Brightwell-cum-Sotwell in South Oxfordshire. Island Farm really is a sanctuary in the truest sense of the word; it is a haven for abused and neglected animals – primarily donkeys, but John never turns away an animal in need – and a place where they can live happily amongst friends, safe in the knowledge that no one will ever hurt them again.

When I first met John I was immediately struck by the incredible connection he has with the animals in his care. When he walks into one of the paddocks at Island Farm, all of the donkeys immediately trot up to him, eager for a stroke or a scratch behind the ears and jostling each other out of the way to get close to him. Each of the eighty donkeys at the sanctuary has received John's undivided care and attention, and in return he has their complete devotion. Without John, many of these beautiful animals would have died of starvation, of wounds inflicted by a cruel owner, of pure neglect. Some would have been deemed worthless and sold for slaughter. For John, no donkey is worthless – each deserves to live a happy, healthy life, with the companionship of other donkeys and the freedom to stretch their legs in a safe environment.

Pollyanne is Island Farm's most famous resident, and what follows is her – and John's – extraordinary story, as told to me during the remarkable time I spent with the team at Island Farm. It was a real honour to see John, Linda, Wendy, Stuart and Gaggy in action – I've rarely seen people work so hard, and with such selfless dedication, for such little material reward. The sanctuary is a labour of love for each and every one of them, and I can only hope that this book allows them to continue doing their vital work for many years to come.

JOHN'S STORY

1

You'll Have to Take the Donkey Too

I was born and grew up in Wantage in the Vale of the White Horse, which is on the borders of Wiltshire and Berkshire and not so very far from where I live now. It was also the birthplace of King Alfred the Great and the poet John Betjeman, but I reckon I've got more in common with another famous son – champion jockey Lester Piggott. There are stables and good riding all around Wantage, so I suppose it's no surprise that both he and I have spent our lives around all things equine ... although he's made a bob or two more than me in the process!

My parents both worked on a local estate, my father as Head Gamekeeper, my mother in charge of the hatchery. Father's job involved training gun-dogs, breeding game birds and protecting them from poachers. My mother had to grade all the eggs that were produced on the estate, check the incubators and care for the chicks. As a boy I enjoyed watching them working and it was clear that they both loved their jobs. But it was hard work and involved long hours – hours during which I was free to roam around and play, alone or with my sister Catherine who was a few years older than me. So we spent our childhoods outdoors, climbing trees, fishing, riding horses. It was a simpler time and we had such freedom back then – a freedom I think few children have nowadays.

I always knew I wanted to work outdoors, like my parents. My first job, age fourteen, was helping the estate workers move felled timber out of the woods. I was just a young lad, so it was my task to clear away the smaller pieces of wood so that the horse-drawn bobs could drive in and be loaded up with the remaining bulk, by burlier men than me. After that I got another job working for a farmer and started saving my wages. They weren't much, but I soon had enough to start up on my own and in my early twenties I started buying and selling ponies. It was a good way for a young man with no ties to make a living; I travelled around, never staying in one place for particularly long, and never felt as if I needed to put down any roots. I was a free spirit. I enjoyed going where the work was, renting stables and fields from farmers, making just enough to get by. Occasionally people would ask me why I didn't get a job that paid better, maybe something in an office? But I would just laugh at the idea. Being stuck inside all day would kill me. I have always belonged in the open air, working with nature.

But as time passed, and even though I was still living the itinerant life of a trader, the pull of family and the idea of settling down started to take hold. I got married, and when my first child was born – a son, Stuart – I held him in my arms and overwhelming love surged through me. I had never experienced anything so powerful, and never imagined I would again ... But I did, just three years later when Neil was born. I was a father twice over: I felt so blessed. As they grew up I taught them all about ponies and encouraged them to ride as soon as they were big enough. They would help me with the grooming after they came home from school and then we would have a kick about with a football before bed.

Before long it became clear that we needed to find a permanent base, a home for my family from which to run my pony business. I'd been saving a little each week the whole of my working life, hoping that one day I'd have enough to buy my own patch of land. I asked my farming friends to keep an eye out and scoured the press and farming magazines to see if there was anything suitable within our price range. After months of searching to no avail, I'd almost given up hope. Nothing I'd found felt right. Then, one day, an old farming mate of mine got in touch. He had heard that there was a tract of land for sale on Frogs Island, in the village of Brightwell-cum-Sotwell, only twenty miles from where I was born. I had nothing to lose, so I decided I'd go and scout it out.

I remember the day I first set foot in the village as clearly as if it was yesterday. It was a weekday so the boys were in school. The sun was shining and I was feeling optimistic: I didn't know what to expect of the place for sale, but from what my mate had said the price was reasonable, which was a good start. I was early, so before making my way to Frogs Island to meet the farmer I decided to have a walk around the village. I parked up outside the village pub, the Red Lion, and set out for a stroll. I took a right, and bumped into a man walking down the middle of the lane with three black Labradors and a little Jack Russell running ahead of him on leads. He nodded and said hello, before going into one of the thatched cottages. A bit further along I was overtaken by a grandmother pushing a toddler in a pram. She seemed to be in great hurry, as if she were very late for something or other. Soon enough I reached a brick building which turned out to be the village hall. I read on the notice board that a playgroup was taking place that morning. I reasoned this must have been where the lady with the pram had been heading. I quickly scanned the other community activities that were held in the hall every week, idly wondering whether Neil would be interested in joining the Scouts, or Stuart the young farmers, were we to live here ... Heading back to the car, virtually every cottage and house I passed was adorned with colourful hanging baskets; there were two quaint little chapels, a proper red phone box – in short, this village looked perfect, and it felt like a real community. I would have to wait to sample a pint in the Red Lion – but if the meeting was a success *and* I liked the local ale, it would be almost too good to be true!

Frogs Island is located on the outskirts of the village. My mate had drawn me a little map to make sure that I found the blink-and-you'll-miss-it turning into Old

Didcot Road. As soon as I pulled up outside the farm-house, Michael, the owner, came out and gave me a wave. He was a strapping man, a few years older than me. He wasted no time in taking me over to see the land he was selling, so I could see what was on offer. 'Frog Island', he explained, was an unofficial name given to his land many, many years earlier, but no one could remember where it got the name in the first place. He suspected the area might have been waterlogged in the past.

Michael wasn't selling up entirely. He was just divid-ing his land in half. The land for sale still looked plenty big enough for my needs, and the price was perfect because I would have enough money left over to build stables for the ponies. I had had a good feeling when I walked around the village, and now I had seen the land I knew I had finally found the place where my family could put down roots. We shook hands and a deal was done. As soon as the paperwork was signed and it was all official, I could move onto the land any time I wanted.

I couldn't wait to tell the family. I had kept it a secret until then because I didn't want them to be disappointed if it didn't work out, but later that night I finally shared the news: we were going to be landowners! They were so excited and immediately set about trying to persuade me to take them for a visit. First of all I told them we had to come up with a name for our farm, one we all liked. 'Frog Island Farm' was already taken by Michael himself, but I still wanted the name to have some link to the local area. After a lot of to-ing and fro-ing – Brightwell Farm? Frog Farm? – the boys and I plumped for 'Island Farm' – simple and memorable!

I didn't have the money to build us a house so we moved into a mobile home on the land instead. The ponies would need a sturdier home, though, so I set about building twenty stables in two rows, with a patch of grass in the middle, surrounded by flower beds. It took me a few weeks, but when they were finished I was proud of what I had achieved. I finally had everything I needed for my pony business to really get going. It didn't take long for the boys to get settled in the village and we soon couldn't remember a time when we'd lived anywhere else. Island Farm was home.

With the new farm I had more room for ponies than I'd ever had before and soon business was booming. I ran riding lessons for local children and Island Farm started to gain a reputation as a good riding school. The boys' mother, Wendy, was a godsend. She took care of all the paperwork and made sure that everything ran smoothly.

Speaking of godsends, some of the local children volunteered to help care for the ponies after school and at weekends. They helped brush them and muck out the stables – it wasn't a glamorous job, but the kids seemed to enjoy it. Cleaning stables requires a pitchfork, a broom, a sturdy wheelbarrow and a strong pair of arms! First, you use the pitchfork to move the manure – the prongs act to sift out the sawdust and straw leaving the manure, which goes straight in the wheelbarrow.

Next, you get your broom and sweep from the front of the stable to the back, so any sawdust and straw is kept well away from the water buckets. It's hard work, but these children seemed to enjoy the opportunity. They loved being around the ponies and their parents were grateful that it stopped them pestering for their own horse. We often found that after a while our volunteers would outgrow it, reach the age when boyfriends and girlfriends were far more interesting than spending weekends knee-deep in manure, but there was always a new group of keen youngsters willing to step into the breach.

One of the children who *did* keep coming back, week after week without fail, was a girl called Linda. She had started helping out when she was thirteen and when her friends gave up she had bucked the trend and carried on. Linda was only small but she worked harder than anyone else and had a real knack with ponies. She had been riding most of her life and eventually she started helping us to teach the younger children how to ride.

Most of the volunteers we had back then were girls but we did get the odd boy who was interested in ponies. John Roberts started helping out when he left school – a big, strong lad who was happy to get his hands dirty. He picked up the nickname Gaggy, I'm not sure how, but it made things simpler than having two Johns around.

I used to buy a lot of my ponies in Wales. There are some good ponies down there, especially in the Valleys. Good jockeys, the Welsh, and (back then, at least) the ponies I bought were often already well trained from being ridden by their owner's children. For me as a buyer, seven or eight years old was the ideal age for a pony – I would find it easier to sell ponies that were experienced, and that had a bit of sense in them. So I would go to Wales in my lorry, buy these ponies, bring them back, get them schooled, get them going, and then sell them on.

I have always loved ponies but back then, as a trader, I didn't really think much about their welfare. I hate to say it now, but all I wanted to do was buy them and sell them on at a profit. Customers would come to me or I would take them to horse fairs and sell them that way. I didn't give a second thought to what lay in store for them beyond that – just as long as I got a good price for them and was putting food on the table for my kids. If I bought a pony and it was in poor health, I would make sure it was rehabilitated before selling it on because that way I'd get a better price.

Quite often the ponies I saw on my travels were in a bad way, particularly during the winter. Their owners often also kept donkeys in wretched conditions, half-starved because they couldn't graze on grass and were fed on the meagre scraps that were all their owners could spare. It was sometimes the case that I could only buy the ponies if I took the donkeys too. I used to spend ages trying to argue my way out of the bind. I really couldn't be doing with donkeys. I didn't want to feed them and house them and take care of them on top of everything else – it would cut into my profits. Inevitably, though, I'd have to relent – it was take the donkeys, or go home empty-handed.

At first I used to give the donkeys to a woman called Miss Philpen who ran a nearby donkey sanctuary. Miss Philpen looked like a little old country lady but she was the type of no-nonsense woman who called a spade a spade – if she didn't like you, you knew about it. But Miss Philpen had a huge heart for donkeys – in 1965 she set up the first donkey sanctuary in the UK, the Helping Hand Animal Welfare League Donkey Sanctuary. Many unwanted donkeys would have starved if it were not for her. When I first knew her, I was just a pony dealer more concerned with himself than with the animals. After dropping the donkeys off at Miss Philpen's, I would take the ponies back to Island Farm. Linda helped me turn ponies that were just skin and bone into strong, healthy beasts. We would make sure the ponies were good riders by using them in lessons we held at the farm. Once we were happy they were fit, we would sell them on.

Giving the donkeys away was a hassle-free option for

me but there were times when I had no choice but to find room for them on the farm. As with the ponies, we would try and get them fit and then sell them. I would try so hard to get rid of them, dropping their prices really low, but while the ponies would get snapped up, the donkeys were always left behind. No one seemed to want them, and before long we were becoming overrun with donkeys and had less room for new ponies. I was paying to feed the donkeys and keep their hooves in good order but simply couldn't make any money from them. It wasn't an ideal situation but there was nothing I could do. I must admit that I found this really infuriating. But my feelings towards donkeys changed once and for all when Jack arrived ...

'Stuart, get the gate! Hurry, lad, where's Gaggy? We need the vet, call the vet!'

I frantically pulled down the ramp on the lorry and ran inside. The donkey was hardly breathing, lying on the straw at the bottom end of the lorry.

'It's okay, boy, we'll get you sorted.' I stroked his muzzle but he was so weak he couldn't even lift his head. His pony companion stood on the other side of the lorry, staring at me as if to say, 'What's all the fuss about?'

I had gone to Wales to pick up a pony, but once I got there the owner told me that his donkey had to go too. I could tell from his face that it would be pointless to argue with him, so I'd nodded even though this was the last thing I needed. The strange thing was I couldn't see any donkey. The owner pointed to the far corner of a sodden field but all I could see was a whole lot of mud and dirt. He pointed again, and this time I saw a tiny flicker of movement in the corner. The donkey was lying down, covered from head to toe in mud. I'd never come across a donkey in such a bad state. He was certainly dying. The owner wasn't going to help me move it – he didn't want to get his jacket muddy. I had come across some hard-nosed types in my time, but I couldn't believe anyone could be so cruel. Five minutes later I was squelching my way back to the lorry with the donkey in my arms and my feet sinking deep into the mud. The poor animal hadn't protested. As I'd lifted him from the ground that would have certainly been his grave if I'd left him there, he just looked up at me, his eyes locking onto mine, wondering what was happening. He was as light as a feather – there was hardly anything to him. I made him as comfortable as I could in the lorry, secured the pony, jumped in the cab and drove home as fast as I could, hoping against hope that he would still be alive at the end of the journey.

He was, just about. Stuart had gone to get the vet and Gaggy was preparing one of the spare stables. I took the sad creature into my arms – I could have waited for the vet but I wanted to get him out of the lorry, where he lay caked in mud, straw and sawdust. I just wanted him to make him clean and comfy: I wanted to help him *live*. No animal deserved to be in such a state.

The vet arrived in a matter of minutes. He told me the donkey had pneumonia, worms and mites. He would need a lot of antibiotics if he was going to survive. I just nodded, I didn't care what it took, or how long, I wanted to see him fit. To this day I don't really know what it was that touched me about this particular donkey – I had seen plenty of animals in poor health before, although none quite so bad. I think it was the look in his eyes when I picked him up that first time: full of trust, even though he had no reason to trust anyone.

Once the vet had given the donkey a strong dose of antibiotics, we cleaned the emaciated animal as best we could and made him comfortable and warm in the stable. I spent a long, anxious night by his side, praying he would make it through until morning. I couldn't bear the thought of him dying here, in my care. Thankfully, he did survive that night, and the next. Over the coming days, with a lot of love, TLC, and plenty of medical attention, he got stronger and stronger.

I didn't usually name the ponies – I knew they wouldn't be staying around for long so there didn't seem much point. But everything changed with my rescue donkey. We bonded so much over the many months it took to get him to good health that I gave him the name Jack.

With Jack, everything was different. There was no way he was going anywhere. And Jack had changed me – I now found I couldn't ignore the other donkeys I came across through my work. Soon they had names, too: Jack was joined by Charlie and Jason. They became my favourites and I began to look forward to spending time with them each day. I cared less and less about buying new ponies to sell on, and started to care more about the welfare of donkeys. I could no longer overlook the fact that it was the donkeys I encountered that seemed to receive the worst treatment.

Watching Jack thrive gave me a feeling of deep accomplishment such as I'd never felt before. I wanted to keep helping these poor creatures and to do something that made a real difference to their lives. Suddenly I didn't care about making a profit any more: caring for animals was what mattered. Convincing my family that we should turn the farm into a donkey sanctuary all those years ago wasn't as big a battle as I expected. I remember talking it over with Stuart one evening over a well-deserved pint in the Red Lion. I was nervous about telling him, but it turned out that he knew what I was going to say before I did and was already on board. He'd long since left school by this point and had been helping out with the ponies his whole life. He knew what the donkeys meant to me and offered to help with the daunting pile of paperwork we'd need to become an official registered donkey sanctuary.

Linda and I started going to lots of markets, particularly the travellers' horse fairs like Appleby and Stow, in search of sick or injured donkeys. If you think that people give sick donkeys away for nothing, think again. We usually had to pay hundreds of pounds for each animal, even if they were so ill they could hardly stand up. I always made sure I had plenty of money in my wallet for these trips – I couldn't bear it if we weren't able to save a donkey just because I was a hundred quid short.

At markets and horse fairs there will usually be several donkeys up for sale. Obviously we can't buy every one we find. So if a donkey looks fit and healthy, we hope that a member of the public will buy them and give them a good home. But if we see a donkey in a bad state, we know that's doubtful. More likely they'll end up in yet another bad home, or with a careless dealer. Or – and this will shock many of you – they will be sold off for Italian salami.

Donkeys that are no longer useful to their owners in the UK are often sold for slaughter, but many people don't realise that donkeys in the UK are slaughtered for salami to be eaten in Italy. Around sixty per cent of salami sold in Italy is donkey meat. All we can do to try and stop this is to try and raise awareness and to buy the sick donkeys we see in fairs to prevent them being sold on for slaughter.

Dealers travel around going to fairs all over the

country, bringing animals for sale from Wales, the Shetland Isles, Scotland ... all over. Some poor creatures have to spend days on lorries, going from sale to sale until they're sold. And this is a serious problem. Plenty of livestock is sold in this way. Which means, sadly, we are kept very busy indeed.

2

Finding Pollyanne

1 March 1997. The day we rescued Pollyanne.

I had a lot to do at the sanctuary that day before we set off for the horse fair – there was a roof that needed fixing and one of the electric fences had been playing up. Salisbury Livestock Market was over seventy miles away and we had to feed and water the donkeys before we left, which meant getting up and out by 5 a.m. Moving the donkeys from their stables into the fields was a time-consuming job back then because they were stabled in pairs or fours. It could take two hours at a time.

I had been up most of the night looking after a sick gelding, so I was feeling pretty tired. I could have easily hit the snooze button on my alarm that morning. But somehow I fought the urge to lie in, swung my legs over the side of my bed and surveyed the room. I saw the mug of tea on the bedside cabinet, stone cold. I had meant to drink it before I fell asleep but my eyes had shut of their own accord, as heavy as lead. My clothes – thick trousers, a grey shirt and a woollen jumper I had been given as a Christmas present many years before – were exactly where I'd left them, draped carelessly over the back of a chair. I leant forward, took the tobacco tin from the trouser pocket, and proceeded to roll my first cigarette of the day. That done, I dressed and made my way to the tiny bathroom to brush my teeth. I have lived in a mobile home for the vast majority of my adult life and I don't think I'll ever live in a house again. I like stepping out my front door and being a few metres from my donkeys, although Stuart doesn't necessarily think it's that good an idea. He used to live onsite but now he's got his own place in nearby Didcot. At the end of a hard day's work he can say goodbye to the donkeys and be on his way – whereas before, when he lived here, he would work late into the night. Stuart is invaluable – while I'm usually out and about in the fields with the donkeys, he's mostly in our little office dealing with paperwork. He deals with all the adoption packs, which is a really important job as without people sponsoring our donkeys we'd have to shut down.

It was a misty morning, and cold, so the donkeys weren't keen to leave their stables. I tied one end of a long rope to the metal gate and the other end to the fence to create a makeshift pathway that would lead the donkeys right to the paddock. I unbolted each wooden stable door one at a time and encouraged the donkeys inside to get going. Usually they just want a stroke from me and then they're happy enough to trot along, but there's always the odd one who will try it on – ducking under the rope to see if they can sneak some extra food, for instance, or heading off in search of a donkey of the opposite sex ... (We neuter the vast majority of donkeys that arrive at the sanctuary as soon as we can, but we still keep them separate. This works well for us and makes things a lot less complicated!) I went from one stable to the next and tried to work as fast as possible, otherwise it would take all day and the donkeys in the final few stables, where the OAPs live, would be extremely fed up by the time I got to them.

Our OAP donkeys are my weak spot. I'm so fond of them because I have been looking after them for so long. The average donkey can live to be fifty years old but rescued donkeys have a much lower life expectancy because of the damage their bodies have suffered over the years. (Jason, one of my original gang, lived to be fifty-seven – the oldest we've ever had. Sadly, we had to have him put to sleep because he went completely blind and started knocking himself about too much. His best friend Lucy is still here, mind you, and she must be nigh-on fifty.) Lots of our elderly donkeys have arthritis and gut problems. Some have suffered strokes. It is possible for a donkey to survive a stroke, but if they can't be saved then sadly we do have to have them put to sleep. Saying goodbye is the hardest part of what I do. Some of my donkeys are like children to me. When Jason passed away, even though he was old and had lived a good life with us at Island Farm, it hurt terribly. I still don't like to talk about it.

Not a lot of people know this, but donkeys often starve themselves to death when they are nearing the end of their lives. They just seem to give up. It is a very painful process that takes several days and if I can, I try to stop it happening. When they are on hunger strike, they won't go near their normal mix (dried peas, beans, wheat and barley) – it holds no appeal – so I offer them little treats; bread covered in honey, doughnuts and hobnob biscuits ... anything to coax them into eating again. If it works I can get them back on their regular diet, and after a few days they might perk up again. But if a donkey is very old and ill, and won't eat anything I try to feed it, then the humane thing to do – more often than not – is to call the vet and have the animal put down. It is less painful than the long-drawn-out alternative.

If the donkey has a close donkey friend, as they often do, then we make sure they are together when the end comes. Watching the exchange between a dying donkey and its companion is so touching. The companion will try to encourage its friend to get up by nuzzling its muzzle until eventually it realises what has happened and understands that it must say goodbye. At this point we leave them alone in the stable, with the door open. When the friend has finished mourning, it will leave the stable voluntarily and go back to the paddock and get on with its daily life. Some will stay in the stable for an hour or two, for others it can take up to two days for them to leave their friend.

Back to the morning in question. Thankfully I found the OAP donkeys as fit as fiddles and I set off to the office to catch up with Stuart and put the kettle on. But as I crossed the yard, I saw Linda had arrived and was ready to set off. I could have done with that cup of tea but no such luck, not if we were going to get to the market to greet the sellers as they arrived ... I'd just have to wait.

That morning as we were about to drive off in our lorry, I remember turning to Linda and asking if she thought it was worth us going. 'Yes,' she said, and smiled because I always ask her this and she always gives me the same answer, no matter what. Even if there's a million and one things we need to do at the sanctuary ... even if our lorry breaks down and we have no transport ... even if I'm really sick ... where there's a donkey in need, there's a will, and where there's a will there's a way.

We arrived at Salisbury Market just before nine and started searching the pens – rows and rows of them filled with cows, sheep, ponies and (every now and again) a donkey or two. It's easy to miss them if you're not careful. I spotted Pollyanne first. She stood at the back, as far away from her owner as possible. Even from a distance I noticed that she had very badly overgrown hooves; amongst the worst I had ever seen. They were curled upwards like clogs – they couldn't have been trimmed for years. They had grown so long that they had began to turn back on themselves; she had to lean backwards to be able to walk at all. When a donkey has bad hooves all the joints, from the hooves to the shoulders, shift out of alignment which can cause a lot of pain and permanent damage. Despite the condition she was in, I'd rarely seen a prettier donkey.

I offered to buy her straight away, but her owner wasn't interested. He was tough-looking, with a face like a pitbull. His arms were folded and he stood a good two feet taller than me. He told me to move on. I ignored him and stayed put: I wasn't going anywhere.

'She's gonna be slaughtered for salami,' he spat. He turned his back and leant on the pen's railings.

'She's too young for that,' I pleaded, trying to win him round. Linda had sensed that I needed to speak to him alone and had walked a pen or two along, but every now and then she glanced back, anxious that something might kick off between us.

'Why do you want her, anyhow?' the guy asked. 'She's no good for anything. Look at her feet, she can hardly walk.'

'I can fix her feet, I've done it before. Give her a chance, she's still young. She deserves a new life,' I pleaded. He seemed to take in everything I was saying but he still wasn't budging.

'I'd get £250 if I sent her for slaughter.'

'Fine,' I replied, 'I'll match it. I'll give you £250 for her.'

He sighed. 'I'm not going to get rid of you, am I?'

'No chance,' I grinned. 'Do we have a deal?'

He reached out a huge greedy hand for the wad of notes I was holding.

'Yeah,' he said. 'But you'll have to load her on your own.'

The second I handed over the money he walked away in the direction of the nearest pub.

We had a Bedford lorry at the time, a seven and a half tonner. We got her in there eventually but we had a heck of a job because of her overgrown feet and because she was so frightened and skittish. She was kicking – she had one hell of a lethal kick – and jumping about, but we got her in the lorry in the end, without losing any of our teeth, and set off for home.

During the drive home I asked Linda what we should call our newest resident – she has a knack for coming up with names.

'Pollyanne,' she replied, without hesitation. 'Pollyanne. I don't know why but she looks like a Pollyanne to me.'

So Pollyanne it was. A pretty name for a very pretty donkey.

3

Slow Beginnings

I turned Pollyanne out in the paddock and she ran away from me as fast as she could. Her legs were going at such a speed, and her feet were so bad, I thought she was going to fall. She stopped by the back fence and turned to face me. Even from a distance I could see that she was shaking, clearly distressed. But I knew she would calm down in the long run. I hate seeing a donkey all panicked and on edge but there is nothing I can do about that – it takes time to build trust and confidence. I walked towards the nearby stables that we keep for new arrivals and picked up a plastic trough and a bucket. I watched her out of the corner of my eye, saw her turn her head downwards and take a mouthful of grass. I slowly walked back and after placing the trough down I poured a bucket full of cold water into it. I was working at the opposite side of the field to Pollyanne but she was studying everything I was doing. I would let her settle in, in a paddock on her own, and come back later.

I carried on with the usual chores – mucking out the boys' stables, repainting the front gate which had faded over the winter, welcoming the afternoon's visitors – but for some reason I couldn't stop thinking about Pollyanne. I kept wanting to rush over and see how she was doing, even though I knew I had to give her space. She had proven in the market that she was a kicker so it would take a long time for her to welcome a stroke and a tickle behind the ears. Still, I couldn't stop thinking what might have happened to her if we'd *not* gone to market that day, or if we'd arrived too late. She would have been sold for slaughter.

Over five thousand ponies and donkeys just like Pollyanne are slaughtered in the UK every year for meat to be sold abroad, for no better reason than they are old or unwanted. Even some racing horses are slaughtered when they end their careers because it costs too much to feed them. This is a common practice often kept hidden from the public eye because the slaughter of ponies and donkeys is a taboo subject. If we hadn't rescued Pollyanne that March day, she would have been loaded onto a lorry and shipped to an abattoir, where she would have been unloaded into a stable to wait for someone to come round and shoot her through the brain with a rifle. The bullets used for killing donkeys and ponies are designed to expand on impact. It makes me shudder to think about it.

Once the donkey or pony has been shot they are lifted up by their hind legs. Their throats are slit through with a knife to allow their blood to drain away. Then a butcher carves up the meat as he or she wishes and the carcass is packaged, ready to transport abroad to Italy or another country. It is no longer legal for live animals to be sent abroad for slaughter so this all takes place in the UK. I do hope that one day slaughtering donkeys and ponies will be banned in this country. Until it is, I will continue to campaign, to raise awareness, and to rescue donkeys destined for the abattoir.

It was almost 4 p.m. by the time I saw Pollyanne again.

I had started leading the donkeys from the first two paddocks back into their stables for the night, and was giving them their dinner. Pollyanne was watching everything but she kept her distance. I carefully unclipped the electric fence rods and stepped inside the paddock, then clipped them back in behind me. I walked slowly towards her, making sure my body language was as relaxed as possible. She stayed where she was until I got within ten metres of her and then she started to move away. I followed her, still moving extremely slowly. She kicked out, even though I was still quite a distance away. I reached down carefully to my jacket pocket and felt for the lump of carrot I had put there earlier. Taking it out, I bent down and threw it onto the ground in front of her. Her eyes focused on it, and then back on me. She took one step forward and grabbed the carrot with her teeth, and then moved back. It made me smile – she was shy all right, but still couldn't resist a piece of carrot.

'I'll see you tomorrow then, Pollyanne,' I said in a quiet voice and began to back away. I continued to face her as I walked backwards, as I didn't want to risk being kicked from behind if she suddenly felt brave. When I was back on the other side of the fence I tossed some mix into a bowl and then lowered it next to the water trough I had put out earlier for her. It was only a small amount of food because I didn't want to overfeed her in case it made her ill.

I knew that if I tried to force her into a stable I would need Linda, Gaggy and Stuart to help me, and ultimately it would cause more harm than good. She would be fine staying in the paddock overnight – it was going to be a dry night, according to the weather forecast, and even if there was a shower she could shelter under one of the trees.

I left her to it and walked over to the final two paddocks to get the last of the donkeys in. They were so glad to see me, pushing each other out of the way to see who could get the closest. Charlie sneaked under the rope, and wandered over to Pollyanne's paddock, eager to get her food, but he couldn't quite reach. He snorted and made his way back to me before I had the chance to tell him off. I quickly ushered him inside his stable with Jack, and locked the door. All the donkeys were safely inside their stables, bar Pollyanne, and I could hear them munching on their mix even through the stable doors.

I was gasping for a cup of tea but first I had to get the chickens in – and we have *a lot* of chickens. We have Anconas, Booted Bantams, Buttercups, Lincolnshire Buffs . . . you name it, we've got it. We have quite a few rescued battery hens too, but they don't tend to live long because of the treatment they've received in the past. I started sprinkling feed outside their coop and in a flash the chickens appeared out of nowhere. I was soon surrounded. The greedier chickens, who couldn't wait, jumped up on top of the feeding cart and started helping themselves. Our chickens are all different sizes, some of the hens are double the size of the cockerels. We must have at least forty chickens, but I can never say exactly how many there are at one time because we are always rescuing more; people frequently bring them to the sanctuary and ask us to take them in.

Our chucks have a large, airy coop to sleep in at night but during the day they roam free, all around the sanctuary. Consequently they lay eggs everywhere – underneath plants, behind the stables, inside the stables, in flower pots ... We'd love to give the eggs to visitors to take home as mementos of their visit, but we can't as we are never one hundred per cent sure when they were laid. We can't risk giving people eggs that might make them ill. I do eat them, though – I'm very partial to scrambled egg on toast.

Once they had finished their dinner they started to hop into their coop, pushing against each other in the race to get the best perch for the night. The larger hens don't half get picked on by the smaller ones! It's as if they don't realise how big they are. Our tiniest hens are really nimble on their feet, they can squeeze through the smallest gaps and make it inside before anyone else.

There are always one or two hens left running around, reluctant to go in for the night. I usually have to chase them for a good five minutes before I can scoop them up and put them inside. I try to outsmart them by doubling back and using a broom to block their escape behind the stables. That must be a funny enough sight at the best of times, but if it's been raining the ground turns to mud and I slip all over the place, like I'm doing a strange dancing routine or something. I've come close to falling on my backside quite a few times. I'd have an audience in stitches, so I'm just grateful that our visitors have gone home by the time I have to go through this rigmarole.

After I'd said goodnight to the chickens I went to see Stuart in the office for a catch-up and a brew. I knew he'd seen Pollyanne as we unloaded her when we got back from the sale, because he'd given us a wave, but I hadn't had chance to talk to him properly and I knew he'd want details. Stuart already had the kettle on – he must have known I'd be gasping. I perched on the end of his desk and began to tell him all about the day.

Stuart began to write up a donkey record card for Pollyanne, with the date, where we rescued her from, and I filled him in on her size and age. There are five categories for donkeys: miniature donkeys are under 9 hands, 9–10 hands donkeys are small standard, over 10–12 are standard, over 12–14 are large standard and over 14 hands are mammoth jacks. Pollyanne was 10.3 hands, standard sized. Pollyanne isn't a pedigree donkey – she's an average grey mongrel donkey, but she was still what I would call a good-looking animal. She was thirteen years old according to her donkey passport, which said she had been born in 1984.

Every donkey, horse, pony and mule in Europe legally needs a passport containing all its details and listing all of its owners, past and present. Nowadays many donkeys are microchipped, in the same way dogs and cats are, but the ordinary old donkey passport featured a silhouette of the donkey with any distinguishing marks draw on by a vet. Pollyanne didn't seem to have any distinguishing marks, unlike some other donkeys that arrive at the sanctuary with heavy scarring.

Stuart finished writing and looked up at me.

'She's in a bad way, awful feet and a terrible kicker,' I told him.

'I know,' he replied, 'I saw her doing her best impression of a buckaroo when you went past before. She's going to be a challenge.'

I explained that she was in the rehabilitation paddock and would be staying there overnight. I also requested that he ask Linda and the others to leave her alone until

I gave them the okay. I wanted her to learn to trust me before I introduced her everyone else. Patience was key if I was to win her round.

'Can you do it?' Stuart asked, knowing the answer.

There has never been a donkey I could not bring round, and if Pollyanne needed years of one-to-one attention then that was what she would get from me. No donkey deserves to live their life in fear. I was determined that one day she would be just as happy as the other donkeys at the sanctuary. I had spent only a short time with her, but I knew that she was very special. It was something in her eyes; when she looked at me, I could see that deep down she was a lovely character. I just had to earn her trust.

I woke up at the crack of dawn the next day. I hadn't had much sleep. I just wanted to know that Pollyanne was okay ... I was worried, I couldn't help it. Even though she hadn't displayed any sign of illness the day before, you never know and I needed to be sure she was in decent health. I got dressed in record time and decided to check on her before breakfast (three rounds of buttered toast, without fail).

I took about five steps from my front door, turned a corner and the paddocks came into view. I could just about make out Pollyanne. The rehabilitation paddock is the furthest field so she was just a hazy grey blob in the distance. I picked up my pace. I walked past the chicken coop and the row of boys' stables and then stopped. She hadn't seen me yet and I wanted to watch her for a while. I leant against one of the wooden fence posts and rolled a cigarette. I saw her move towards the water trough I had left her and she took some water. It was early morning so there was hardly a sound, just the odd bird tweeting. Even the donkeys in the stables behind me were being quiet for a change. Once she'd had as much as she wanted to drink, she walked over to the left-hand side of the paddock and started munching on some grass. She ate slowly, glancing up every now and again. She stayed there for five minutes or so and then moved towards the middle of the paddock. I remained as still as possible as I didn't want her to see me but when I flicked the wheel on my lighter she turned and I could have sworn she looked straight at me. I held my breath. She didn't react, she just carried on eating. I exhaled. She was a pretty little thing but those hooves were awful. They definitely needed sorting out as soon as possible; but first I would have to address her kicking issues, otherwise I would end up with concussion.

I sighed, and made my way back to the mobile. I needed to eat a good breakfast because I had a big day ahead. A film crew from *Pet Rescue* were due at nine to interview us about Loppy, a donkey we had rescued a few months earlier, and I had to make sure that all the donkeys were out in the paddocks, watered and fed by the time they arrived.

I had just swallowed my last piece of toast when Gaggy stuck his head round the door, asking whether I was ready. He'd prepared the donkeys' mix in the cart so he was all ready to go. In the mornings we feed the mix to the female donkeys and OAPs, and we leave the boys to graze. If we give them mix in the morning it makes them a bit hyper – I don't know why – so we wait until the evening.

Gaggy and I chatted as we walked along. He asked about the horse sale and I told him about Pollyanne. He wanted to know whether there had been other donkeys there in need of rescue, but I explained that Pollyanne had been the only one in desperate need. We could only hope all of the other healthy horses and ponies had gone to good homes.

We worked together, falling into our familiar routine. I filled the feeding troughs and he refilled the water bowls. When we got to Loppy's stable I told him to go on without me while I readied her for her big TV debut. I gave her a handful of mix to keep her occupied long enough for me to put her collar on without her trying to make a quick getaway. I tied one end of a rope to her collar and led her outside before tying the other end of the rope to the stable door. Then I could get on with grooming.

I enjoy spending one-on-one time with the donkeys, grooming them. I find it very therapeutic and I reckon they enjoy it too. Some of the donkeys will have never been groomed before they arrive at our sanctuary so it can be a bit of a challenge the first couple of times. Now, Loppy will nudge another donkey out of the way if it means she can get close to a bristled brush or sponge.

First, I shampooed her, rubbing in the specially formulated shampoo with a rough sponge. (We don't have giant bath tubs for donkeys, I'm afraid.) Then I brushed her using a bristled brush to remove all the dirt she had picked up from the paddocks and stables. Then I rinsed her off using a big hose – Loppy is a real water baby – being careful to wash any shampoo away from her eyes. Next I used a 'sweat scraper' to take the excess water off her coat because I don't want any donkey catching a chill or worse. Sweat scrapers look similar to the scrapers you use to get ice off a car's windscreen – they do a great job and in a matter of minutes Loppy was as dry as a bone.

For her face and legs I use a soft brush. When I brush

her face, I let her lean her head on my shoulder. I have to be careful she doesn't get too relaxed or she could easily fall asleep! Loppy doesn't mind me brushing her tail but some donkeys aren't as comfortable having their tails touched – especially if they have been abused in the past. Loppy really is a softie, though. I used a hoof pick to clean the dirt from her hooves and then give them a quick polish. For a finishing touch I add a few squirts of conditioning spray to make her coat glossy. All in all it takes me about twenty minutes to groom a donkey. I could be even quicker but I like to do it right, and I don't believe in cutting corners. Grooming is a great way of building up trust with a donkey: you shouldn't rush it.

As I was finishing up, I saw an assortment of cars and a van pull up in the car park. The van had the Channel 4 logo running up its side so I knew it was the people from *Pet Rescue*. They started unloading various cameras, tripods and miles of wires. To be honest it made me feel a bit nervous. I'd expected just a presenter and a cameraman. Guessing they'd be a while, I led Loppy into one of the smaller paddocks, and took off her head collar. 'Go on, girl,' I said, and off she went, nibbling on some grass and stretching her legs. In the rehabilitation paddock opposite, Pollyanne was doing the same thing. I walked over to where Gaggy had left the mix cart, took a cup-sized amount and poured it in to Pollyanne's feeding bowl. I watched as she took a step closer, then stopped. She clearly wanted the food but she didn't want to go near me. I took two steps back, and she took one step forward, so I took another two steps back again she took one step forward – we carried on doing this until Pollyanne reached the feeding bowl. She started eating and I slowly moved closer, one step at a time. I managed to get within five metres of her without her darting off – quite an achievement. As I watched her, I took in her coat, so dirty and matted. She'd probably never been groomed in her life.

'Mr McLaren?'

The lady's voice made me jump. Pollyanne was startled too and retreated.

'Is that Loppy?' she asked, pointing at Pollyanne. I laughed.

'No, that's Pollyanne. Loppy's over here.'

The TV crew were taken aback by Loppy. She is huge – 14.2 hands – and is dapple grey in colour. Her ears are nearly eighteen inches long, which means she's a record breaker. If there's another female donkey in England with ears as big as hers, we've yet to find her. The *Daily Mail* actually did challenge the nation to do just that but Loppy's ears were just too big to have any competition!

I explained to them how a sympathetic horse dealer had bought Loppy at a livestock market in Southall, Greater London, and brought her to us. She had been in a terrible state. She had been living in Scotland, so she must have had to travel hundreds of miles that day and she could well have ended up being bought by another, more unscrupulous, owner. Thankfully, the man who saved her knew about us, and knew we would take care of her.

Loppy looked different to any other donkey we had ever seen – her loppy ears were naturally the inspiration for her name – and shortly after her arrival at the sanctuary we did some research to try and pinpoint what type of donkey she was. We read all our various donkey books, asked our friends from the donkey world and eventually found out that she is an Andalucían, or Cordobese, donkey – an extremely rare breed. They come from the valleys of the Guadalquivir in Spain. There are only 120 donkeys of this breed left in the world; there is a real threat of their extinction unless something is done to prevent it.

Pet Rescue was then a new daytime show on Channel 4 – it followed the work of RSPCA inspectors and animals that had been rescued. The presenter was a big animal lover and enjoyed getting up close and personal with the donkeys. I introduced her to Winston, who had a really bad deep scar by his ears. Our vet believed that his previous owner had cut his ears with a Stanley Knife. Winston is okay now but the TV crew were shocked to think that someone could treat an animal so badly. He readily approached the presenter for a cuddle even though he had never met her before.

Pet Rescue was a family show so we couldn't talk too much about the abuse some of the donkeys had suffered. Instead, they showed some 'before' photos of donkeys that had arrived in an awful state, some of them just skin and bone, and followed them up with footage of them in the paddock, happy and well cared for. They were filming for so long that it was almost dark before they decided to head off. I must admit I was excited at the prospect of seeing the end result: it would be Island Farm's TV debut and more than anything I hoped that the publicity would bring rewards.

As soon as the convoy had disappeared from view out of the car park I headed over to Pollyanne's paddock. I had managed to feed her at lunchtime while the crew were tucking into some of the Red Lion's best grub, but I'd been so busy showing them round all afternoon that I hadn't had a chance to feed her again. She was waiting at her feeding trough when I arrived, as if to tell me to hurry up!

I poured some mix into her bowl and instead of running off as she had before, she stayed put. I was only an arm's stretch away from her, and I forgot for a moment how much of a kicker she was. She looked as if butter wouldn't melt, but the second I moved my hand up to my face to scratch my nose she kicked out and knocked the trough over, spilling water everywhere. I was just relieved that she caught the container and not my leg. I couldn't say for certain that Pollyanne had been hit in the past but it was a strong possibility. She carried on kicking out, but I just stayed still and eventually she moved off.

I had lost my bottom teeth a few months earlier, trying to put a head collar on a donkey. The poor donkey was so startled, she lifted her head too quickly and hit me right in the mouth. I can still remember the pain and the taste of blood. I had covered my mouth with my hands and tried to stop myself from bursting into tears.

Gaggy was with me and I didn't want him to tell the others I was a cry baby. Once the gums stopped bleeding and I could I survey the damage, I realised each of the front four teeth was wobbling. I didn't want to go the dentist so I just left them as they were. Two weeks later I was tucking into pie and chips when they fell out, landing right in my dinner! It was a good job I felt them drop, otherwise I could have choked on them! Oh yes, it can be a dangerous occupation indeed. I'm proud of the fact that I've never broken a bone – although I've had some close shaves. Knock on wood, eh?

The next few weeks with little Pollyanne were a challenge to say the least. She would try to kick me whenever she could. I gave her space for a while but she couldn't stay out in torrential rain for too long – it would have made her ill – and eventually the day came when I had to move her to the stables. It wasn't pretty and she certainly made her feelings clear. Thankfully, Gaggy and Linda were on hand to help and we managed it together.

Pollyanne was definitely learning to trust me, but very tentatively. I was still a long way from persuading her to let her guard down. We put her in a stable with Betty, a brown donkey I had rescued two years previously. She was older than Pollyanne and we hoped she would be a calming influence. I was delighted to see that Pollyanne seemed to take to her instantly. The second she got through the stable door she walked over to Betty and gave her the usual donkey greeting – a quick sniff followed by blowing at the nose. (Don't ask me why they do this, they just do!) Although Pollyanne had probably lived a solitary existence up until then, all donkeys like company. They're not happy living on their own. We closed the door and left them to it. It was late and we all deserved a pint but none of us had the energy to change out of our soaking, mud-splattered clothes so we said goodnight and headed our separate ways.

The next morning I got up extra early and raced to the stable to check on Pollyanne and Betty before the others arrived. I opened the door slowly and peered into the shadows. I could make out Betty at the back but I couldn't see Pollyanne. Where was she? I opened the door wide and stepped inside. To my surprise, when Betty turned to face me, another face appeared just over her shoulder. Pollyanne! She had been standing right beside to her and seemed just as happy as could be. Realising that I hadn't come bearing food, Betty immediately lost interest in me and instead turned back to her new friend. I beamed from ear to ear, a big and genuine smile: Pollyanne didn't need to be alone any more.

By the time the others arrived I'd already fed the girls, let the boys into the front paddocks and released the chickens. Gaggy and Linda looked at me in amazement.

'Exactly what time did you get up this morning?' Gaggy asked, knowing that I must have been working for a good hour and a half at least. 'I could have had an extra hour in bed if I'd known you'd have done all this, I was so tired after last night's shenanigans.'

'Come and see this,' I said, shrugging off his comment, and led them both to Betty and Pollyanne's stable where I'd left the top of the door open so we could just peer in without disturbing them.

'I don't believe it,' Linda exclaimed the second she saw them. The bucking donkey we'd been chasing around the paddock was gone; instead, Pollyanne was lovingly grooming Betty, nibbling at her neck and shoulders – and, even more astonishing, allowing Betty to do the same to her.

With everyone in such a good mood, I thought it was a good time to talk through my plans for Pollyanne. The next stage, as I saw it, was for Pollyanne to be able to mix with other donkeys. She'd been at the sanctuary for a few weeks now, and I felt I could begin by letting her and Betty into the paddock with the OAPs. With the older donkeys she wouldn't get as overwhelmed as she would if she went in with the younger girls, who can get very excitable when a new donkey arrives on the scene. Linda and Gaggy trusted me and agreed with my plan, although I could tell they were nervous that Pollyanne wasn't ready to be integrated.

To prepare the way, we tied a rope from the stable door to the fence post, so Betty and Pollyanne would have to turn right out of the stable – they then only had the choice of going into the paddock or into a dead end at the bottom at the stable block. Betty knew the routine well and after a 'Come on, girl!' from me, she trotted out of the stable, Pollyanne hot on her heels, and the two of them made their way nicely into the paddock. Betty went straight up to Gloria, Elsie and Dot as if to say hello and introduce Pollyanne. After a couple of *hee-haws* and a bit of sniffing, they wandered off and started eating grass.

I turned to Linda. 'That went well!' I remarked but Linda just laughed.

'You've not got her back in yet. It's getting them in that's the difficult part, not letting them out!'

She was right, and five hours later I returned, feeling a bit apprehensive. I opened the gate and called to the group. Donkeys tend to follow each other in a line, and that's exactly what happened: first was Elsie, then Dot, then Gloria, Betty and, finally, Pollyanne. To my amazement she ran straight into her stable and went over to her feeding bowl and started tucking in. She didn't even try to kick me as she trotted past – another improvement on the day before.

As time went by, Pollyanne got better and better and eventually started letting me stroke her. I always watched her body language like a hawk, though, and if she tensed up I moved away quickly. A lot of the time I let her come to me, usually following the others who wanted some attention. She was still in a paddock away from the general public, so she had to get used only to me and, on the odd day I wasn't around, Linda.

Shortly after Loppy's TV debut on *Pet Rescue*, we got a phone call asking whether we had four donkeys that would be available to appear in a kids' TV show the BBC were filming. They needed four donkeys for the second episode of *The Phoenix and the Carpet*, an adaptation of the E. Nesbit novel. They needed donkeys that wouldn't be fazed by the hustle and bustle, as the scene would be set in an Indian bazaar. I had read *Five Children and It* when I was a lad and this was the sequel – I was never much of a reader but I enjoyed the escapades of Cyril, Anthea, Robert, Jane and the Lamb, so this would be an exciting day out. I chose Charlie, Chocolate, Jack and Ben for the job – Loppy had already had her five minutes of fame.

I travelled with Gaggy to the location, leaving Linda and Stuart to run things at the sanctuary. All the donkeys coped so well with the journey and I hoped they would be as well behaved on set. It was definitely a new experience for them, that's for sure. And me! The set was incredibly busy and noisy, with people rushing about all over the place – this way and that. They all looked very important but I couldn't tell you what any of them were actually doing! We were well looked after, but I thought it would be a good idea to stay as far out of the way as possible until we were needed. When it came time to go onto the set, it really was like being in an exotic bazaar.

We were surrounded by colourful fabrics and tempting fruits – poor Jack didn't understand that the food he had his eye on was plastic; just a prop. Chocolate was most alarmed by the huge yellow Phoenix (which was made of soft plastic and feathers). He had never seen anything that odd looking at Island Farm, and when it spoke he looked very confused!

In spite of all the new sounds, sights and smells, the donkeys behaved very well indeed and did us proud. They spent most of their time in the background but they did get to interact with the child actors and they all acquitted themselves beautifully. It was a very long day but I must admit it seemed to tire me out more than the donkeys. When we arrived back at the sanctuary they trotted down the ramp as fast as they could, heading for their stables. It was well past dinner time so I was surprised to see Linda still doing the rounds. She'd been held up by Pollyanne, who was refusing to come in – it was getting dark and I could just about make her out in the corner of the paddock. I was worried that she had lapsed back to her kicking ways, but Linda reassured me that she hadn't tried to lash out, she'd just backed away every time Linda had tried to encourage her to go forward. I couldn't understand it.

I unbolted Pollyanne and Betty's stable door. Betty was inside, munching on her mix. She had no intention of leaving until the morning. Once the door was open I made my way to the paddock and opened the gate.

'Pollyanne!' I called out, more for myself than for her. It had grown so dark that I couldn't see her at all.

'Pollyan—' Before I could finish she appeared through the darkness, and rubbed her head against my body. I couldn't believe it! I stroked her, thinking she would bolt, but she stayed put, nudging me again for another cuddle. It was as if she was a completely different donkey. I must have stroked her for a good ten minutes before Linda came out of the barn and Pollyanne took a step away. Looking straight at me, she proceeded to trot into her stable. Without a word of encouragement from me. I was gobsmacked. I followed her, stuck my head through the door and saw she had settled in the corner next to Betty, and was eating her mix. Linda couldn't believe it either.

'She messed me around for close to two hours. Two hours! And then you arrive and she goes straight into her stable. I don't understand it!'

Linda tried to look furious but she couldn't pull it off. We both burst out laughing.

'I honestly think she was waiting for me,' I explained. 'She wanted to check I was back okay.' I was almost choked up by Pollyanne's reaction to my return. I've seen donkeys in all sorts of states over the years: some worse than Pollyanne and with worse tempers, but I'd never seen one turn around so quickly. There really was something special about Pollyanne – she had a gentle soul, and even though she had no reason to trust a human being ever again, she had put her faith in me.

'Right, well, that's me put in my place,' Linda said, with a smile as she wandered off towards the car park.

'You better not be leaving us on our own again ... Pollyanne'll start to pine!'

The next morning I woke up feeling extremely optimistic. The day before had been enjoyable for a whole host of reasons, but the highlight had been witnessing Pollyanne's final transformation from a frightened, cowed creature into a donkey who actually sought out and loved attention from a human. From me! Just a few months earlier, that had been unthinkable.

Her feet were still in a terrible state. I hadn't tackled them yet for fear of ending up with a head injury but when Linda arrived I told her my plan: today was going to be the day I sorted them out.

After we'd let the boys and girls into their retrospective paddocks and released the chickens from their coop, I went to see Pollyanne. I opened the stable door, half expecting her to be annoyed because I'd already let Betty out half an hour before, but she seemed quite content to let me attach her collar without any fuss. I led her out, and she walked as gracefully as a donkey with bad feet can. Her body was still leaning back, which was hard to watch, but I knew it would right itself once her feet were under control. I tied one end of the rope to the stable door and called for Linda's help. I was Pollyanne's favourite, but she had learnt to trust Linda too and I hoped she would be distracted by the carrot in Linda's hand while I worked on her hooves.

Most donkeys need their feet trimming every six to ten weeks, but it must have been years since Pollyanne's were last seen to. I was initially concerned that it would be too painful for her to stand still while I lifted her hoof to trim it – sometimes, if a donkey has really bad joints or arthritis, you have to trim them on the floor. Thankfully, though, Pollyanne wasn't in that much dis-comfort when I lifted her feet so I was able to do it that way. She didn't object too much to me touching her feet because she was busy munching on the carrot – I knew that old trick would work! I laid out all my tools so I had them all to hand. I have a couple of knives – a loop knife and a short blade; a rasp (which is the farrier's version of a cheese grater); and some half-round nippers (pliers).

To start with I removed all the mud and dirt from Pollyanne's foot, so I could have a good look at the state of her hoof underneath. I knew I had to remove all the excess hoof tissue that was sticking out at the front of her foot – the growth that made her look like she was wearing a clog. Because the foot hadn't been touched for a long time it really was a mess but using my tools I started trimming and shaping the hoof so it started to look more like it should. To shape a hoof I begin at the heel and work outwards. A novice would need to concentrate on checking the position of the pedal bone, but I reckon I must have trimmed over ten thousand donkey feet over the years – I could almost do it blind-folded. With Pollyanne, I worked as fast as I could, finishing one foot and moving on to the next with as little fuss as possible. By the time I'd finished, she was getting a bit fidgety but that was mostly because she wanted to be in the paddock with her friends. And she hadn't made even the slightest flicker of a move to kick out.

Thanking Linda for helping me, I led Pollyanne to the paddock and took off her collar. She gave her head a quick shake and took a few steps. She wasn't one hundred per cent sure of her new feet, as her hooves were now at a different angle, but she seemed happy enough. She was still leaning back out of habit but I knew that in a matter of weeks she would start to correct her posture. I knew there was a risk of lasting damage to her joints. I still worry about that, but I have to keep my fingers crossed that she won't develop bad arthritis in the future.

I looked from Pollyanne over to the rehabilitation paddock, where a brown-grey donkey called Starlight was now standing. Starlight was a tiny little thing we had rescued two weeks earlier from a travellers' fair. Starlight had been in a worse physical state than Pollyanne when she arrived, with awful cuts all over her back and rump. At the fair, I had been overwhelmed by the horror of it all and just had to get her as far away from her abusive owner as possible.

'Morning, Starlight.' I spoke quietly as I walked towards her.

She came over to me, slowly. Despite the awful treatment she'd received in the past, she was beginning to come out of her shell a bit. In the first days of her arrival, I had cut off a lot of her hair, as it had grown matted and the cuts were beginning to get infected. Far from resisting my attention, she had let me tend to her wounds without complaint. There's a dignity in that.

Starlight walked with me to the water tap by the side of the stables and watched as I took the soft cloths I used to clean her wounds out from my pockets. Our vet had taken a look at her when she had first arrived and said that as long as I kept all the cuts clean they should heal over fine. They were almost healed now, and she hadn't needed any stitches as I had first thought. Once I'd finished cleaning, I gave her a quick tickle under her chin and sent her on her way. She was nervous around Linda and Gaggy, and still seemed afraid of other donkeys so she would be staying in the rehabilitation paddock for a little while longer.

Pollyanne had been watching me with Starlight and as I headed for the office for a cup of tea I heard her bray for me. I turned and waved. 'I'll be back soon, Pollyanne!' Pollyanne just stared at me, then slowly went back to the others who were busy grazing. I heard Duncan bray in an adjacent paddock and couldn't help but laugh. Duncan is a donkey we rescued from a field overlooking the M1 motorway. He had been on his own for years before his owners reluctantly handed him over to us. When he arrived at the sanctuary he was so overjoyed at seeing fellow donkeys again that he wouldn't stop braying at them – he still does it all day long sometimes. I'm sure some of the older donkeys move to the far side of their paddock just to get some peace and quiet. He's definitely our noisiest donkey. Duncan brayed again at Pollyanne but when he got no response, he moved on to talk to some visitors and got his back stroked in return.

I just about managed to get myself a cup of tea and a

ham sandwich before Simon our vet arrived in his Land Rover. Simon and his colleague Roger have been looking after my ponies and donkeys for years. They only charge us a nominal amount because we're a charity, and they're always on call in case of emergency. I've lost count of the number of times I've been standing in a muddy paddock with Simon at silly o'clock in the morning, or rushed to his surgery with an injured donkey we've rescued that needs urgent attention.

'All right, John,' Simon said as he stepped through the office door. He's a big lad, prop forward for the local rugby team, so he struggles to manoeuvre himself around the cramped office. 'Having a slow day I see,' he said, pointing at me in my swivel chair with a sandwich in my hand. He likes to joke that I sit around all day doing nothing, while Linda and Gaggy do all the work. 'What've you got for us today, then?' he enquired, with his work bag in his hand.

'Three castrations,' I replied. 'They're in the top paddock, clueless as usual.'

When we rescue donkeys we always castrate the stallions unless there is a very important reason not to. Stallions can be hard to control and aggressive if a nearby female is in heat but once they are castrated, they calm down a great deal. We have too many female donkeys to have frisky stallions walking around – the last thing we want are lots of foals, or fights breaking out between the lads.

Usually Simon can castrate a donkey in the field, weather permitting. He first has to inject the donkey to knock it out. It usually takes about fifteen minutes from when the donkey is asleep to complete the castration. Afterwards they bleed a tiny bit, but I keep an eye on them and they are usually fine and dandy after a couple of days. We always make sure he does it when there are no visitors around – it's not a very dignified process for the poor fellows so we try to save them from too much embarrassment!

It can take them a while to lose their macho tendencies but once they have calmed down I introduce them to the main group of boys. The group soon deal with any new arrivals with ideas above their station – most regularly the smaller donkeys. Rocky and Samson are the main leaders of the group. Rocky is a grey donkey aged about twenty and Samson is a large brown-grey donkey a year or two older. They are the ones that the others follow around, and they're both as soft as a brush.

The boys' group has donkeys from all over the world. We've got German donkeys, Hungarian donkeys and we think that our biggest donkey, Nigel, is from Romania but we're not sure. He's very tall and towers over me and Gaggy. They were all brought over to the UK to be sold for slaughter, but we rescued them and gave them a chance of a good life. When they arrive they don't understand any of my commands because to them I'm speaking in the wrong language but after a while they pick it up from watching what the others do. I'd love to know for sure where Nigel is from, so if we ever get a visitor from Romania I'm going to ask them to speak to him and I can watch to see if his ears prick up at any of the words.

From time to time we let rehabilitated donkeys go out to foster homes, but having rescued them from terrible circumstances and put so much time and effort into making them well again, I am very careful to make sure that they go to loving – and safe – homes. I would never let a donkey go to a foster home on its own because they need companionship so I prefer to let a bonded pair go together. I'm very thorough when approving people. I visit them at home, interview them numerous times and only when I'm one hundred per cent happy do I let someone take a pair of our donkeys. I make sure we set up regular times to visit so that I can check the donkeys are still happy, sometimes for years afterwards. People joke that it is easier to be chosen as Sir Alan Sugar's next apprentice than it is to get the thumbs-up to foster a donkey from me.

Our fostered donkeys are scattered right across the

UK: Dolly and Dimbles are fostered in Devon, Toppy and Chief are fostered in Gloucestershire, and Grover and Trooper are fostered in Buckinghamshire. Callan went as a companion to a donkey in South Wales, and they're completely smitten with each other. Nowadays we run special training classes at the sanctuary so that people can learn how to care for donkeys – it's not just a case of dumping a donkey in a field and leaving it to fend for itself. With the right education, attitudes are slowly changing. We invite vets, donkey owners, people who would like to own donkeys in the future and animal lovers to attend our classes, run in partnership with the Donkey Sanctuary in Sidmouth, Devon.

4

The Understudy

'Are you ready, Dad? It's time for us to get going.'

I could hear Stuart calling me. It was a hot summer's day and we were heading for the local steam rally, but I still needed to grab my jacket just in case it poured down the second we arrived. I was wearing my best showing suit – everything had been pressed and polished, I had my cap in my hand and I'd brushed my hair; I looked as smart as I possibly could and I wasn't about to let a bit of weather mess it all up.

I looked out the window of the caravan and could just about make out Pollyanne having a rub-down by Gaggy in the yard. Pollyanne had been with us for a full year now, and I was so pleased with how much she had come on. She lapped up any attention the visitors gave her and was one of the gentlest donkeys we had ever had. She was more than happy to let the others handle her now, but we still had a special connection.

'I'm here now,' I grumbled as I reached Stuart. 'Just hold these while I turn my sleeves up,' I said, handing him my hat and jacket. He sighed, knowing that there was no way I could sit in a hot lorry for two hours with a long-sleeved shirt restricting me. I don't exactly like dressing up formally, but with the sleeves rolled up I feel better about everything.

'Have you loaded the girls up yet?' I asked.

'I hope you don't mean us,' Wendy joked. Linda was staying behind to look after the donkeys and Wendy would be manning the phone and welcoming any visitors while we were away. We wouldn't be back until about eight o'clock, so they'd have a full day ahead of them.

'Well, unless you want to spend the day being stroked and tickled by tourists, I think we better stick with Queen and Sophie,' I smiled.

'Well, we seem to have a problem there,' Stuart said. 'Sophie doesn't seem to want to come along today. She wouldn't let us lead her in.'

I carried on walking to the lorry and saw that Sophie was standing outside while Queen was happily munching on some straw inside. We never force a donkey to do something it doesn't want to. Some people think that's daft but I figure that our donkeys have put up with abuse and neglect for years and the least they deserve now is not to be pushed and pulled in ways they don't want. They deserve to be treated with respect.

'Never mind, Sophie,' I whispered, patting her mane. 'You can have the day off.'

'But we can't just go the rally with one donkey, they'll be so disappointed.' Stuart looked worried.

'Don't flap, Stuart, I've got a plan. Give me two minutes.'

I ran round the corner to where Gaggy was finishing up with Pollyanne. 'Wait up,' I shouted as he began to lead her back to the paddock. A second later I was by her side.

'So, Pollyanne, how do you fancy coming out for the day?' I asked as I stroked her muzzle. She nudged upwards as if to say, 'Yes please!'

'Come on then, Queen's waiting.' I took hold of her collar but I needn't have bothered, she trotted happily all the way to the lorry and up the ramp.

'Are you sure about this?' Stuart asked.

'Never been surer of anything in my life. Pollyanne's ready to go out into the big world.'

When we travel to an event such as a steam show or a fête it's usually two or three of us, with two donkeys to show. The day of the steam rally, our troupe comprised me, Stuart, Pollyanne and Queen. We do these events to let people know who we are and what we do, and to raise money to help feed the donkeys for the next week or two. People come up to meet and make a fuss of the donkeys, and then maybe sign up to sponsor a donkey or drop a few coins in the donation box.

As we parked up in our designated spot and set up the pen, I couldn't help but feel a tiny bit nervous. It was the first time we'd been to this particular event and I hadn't expected it to be so big. The visitors hadn't arrived yet but the sheer number of exhibitors was enough to throw me. There was a fun fair too, which would be swarming with people the second the gates opened at 10 a.m.

I led Pollyanne and Queen down the ramp. Queen was well used to the drill and led the way into the pen. They both seemed happy enough and soon settled in, tucking into the mix we had brought with us. I left them to it and started arranging the adoption leaflets on a small wooden table.

As soon as the fair opened, the pen was surrounded

by people wanting to stroke Pollyanne and Queen. People of all ages love donkeys. I was quizzed by a little boy who wanted to know what the donkeys like to eat and an older lady who wanted to know Pollyanne's story.

'Gosh, that's awful!' the lady exclaimed when she heard about the state Pollyanne was in. 'Pass me an adoption form – I simply must help.'

Pollyanne seemed to like the fuss and attention. She wasn't affected by the children shouting, the organs playing or the occasional balloon flying into her pen. Halfway through the day Queen went to the back of the pen so she could have a rest away from the visitors, but Pollyanne stayed at the front, moving from person to person. She loved it and lapped up the attention. She seemed almost disappointed when it was time for her to go back in the lorry and fixed me with her most doleful expression.

'Come on, girl, you can come on another trip soon,' I said, as I gave her one last pat.

Pollyanne had really done me proud.

Back at the sanctuary, I parked up and started unloading the girls. Linda and Wendy rushed over.

'So . . . how did it go?' said Linda tentatively.

'Perfect. Just perfect,' I said. I couldn't stop smiling. 'She's a complete natural.'

Linda and Wendy were over the moon. They had been on pins all day wondering what was going to happen, both secretly imagining Pollyanne would revert to her old ways in public and create a scene. It was good to know that she could be trusted to behave herself in public and that we could rely on her to help us drum up support to keep her home going.

Before I could lead Pollyanne back into her stable with Betty, Linda pulled me to one side and said she wanted a word. Had I noticed, she asked me, that Betty had been spending more and more time with a little brown donkey called Dolly? When she said that, I knew she was getting at something I already knew deep down myself: Pollyanne could never be Betty's soulmate. That sounds soft, I know, but donkeys really do pal up for life with a friend and you can't force it. They choose their own soulmate just as we do. Betty and Pollyanne had certainly become good friends since sharing a stable – but once they joined the other girls they started spending less and less time together. Betty had started hanging out with Dolly, and almost straight away it was clear to me that they were really bonding.

Lots of the donkeys on Island Farm have soulmates. There's Charlie and Jack, Holly and Emily, Franco and Sennan. Sometimes they arrive already paired up, some donkeys pair off the second they set eyes on each other – like a lightning bolt in a romantic movie – and for others it's a gradual thing that happens over a period of several months.

I hadn't said anything to the others but when Linda confirmed my own suspicions I knew it was time to stop denying it. I had so badly wanted Betty to be Pollyanne's perfect companion but it wasn't to be. I couldn't help but wish Pollyanne would find her soulmate here at the sanctuary, but I knew I had to be patient. Pollyanne had friends she liked to mix with in the paddock like Lilac and Tilly-Mint and she was happy enough for the time being.

'Never mind, Pollyanne,' I said and gave her a gingernut biscuit I had been hiding in my jacket all day. She didn't really understand what I was going on about – she was a contented little thing and truth be told I got the impression that she liked spending time with me more than the other donkeys. I'd lost count of the times I'd gone into the office to have a cuppa and seen her face pressed up against the glass door, as if to say, 'What about me?' Once, I offered her a lukewarm cup of tea to see what she would do. She took one sip and spat it out. Donkeys are not partial to tea as a rule, but Queen loves it. If I ask her whether she would like a cup of tea she rolls her top lip up as if to say, 'Gasping, don't mind if I do.' It makes for a crowd-pleasing party trick.

I settled Pollyanne in a paddock with the other girls and then headed to the far paddock to mend the emergency stable. We keep that particular stable free at all times so that if a donkey injures itself or has a stroke in the night we can keep it separate from the others until the vet arrives to treat it. It is also useful if a donkey comes to us heavily pregnant, as it can house a foal safely and in relative tranquillity. The wind had been so wild the previous evening that part of the roof had been ripped off. Thankfully there were no donkeys in there at the time, but it urgently needed fixing in case we had cause to use it any time soon.

As I stood at the top of my ladder and hammered new nails into the wood, I felt like a bird perched on top of a tree, the hustle and bustle of the sanctuary spread out before me. There was Linda shovelling manure into a wheelbarrow, Gaggy was repairing a puncture on his van, I could see Wendy in the office on the phone and Stuart was in the kitchen washing up some cups from earlier. The donkeys were all quietly grazing in their different paddocks, apart from Barron who was chasing a plastic bag around – he'll obsess over anything that the wind blows in his direction. He picked up the plastic bag by its handles and swung it around, delighted by the crinkling noise it made. Pollyanne was having a drink in the water trough. Queen was grooming one of the smaller brown donkeys with her teeth.

All I could think was how lucky I was. Other people might have millions in the bank but I had a job I love with all my heart, a great family and fantastic friends. The things money really can't buy.

A few months passed, and then a call came through from the theatre in Henley-on-Thames. The publicity department wanted a donkey to promote a play at the Kenton Theatre. The job entailed being led through the streets wearing a small advert, and interacting with people who might never have thought about visiting the theatre before. Did I have a suitable candidate? I did indeed. I knew straight away that Pollyanne would love to do it.

The Kenton Theatre has been around since 1805 and is the oldest theatre in Oxfordshire. When we arrived, I saw that it was across the road from a lovely pub and on the same street as a brewery – I'd have liked to have sampled some of their wares en route, but I suspected we probably wouldn't have time: we had a job to do. Pollyanne and I made our way to the theatre's main entrance, her hooves clip-clopping on the pavement. I was just admiring the red paintwork and golden masks that adorned the doorway when it opened and a lady dressed from head to toe in black appeared. She looked straight past me and instead greeted Pollyanne.

'You're perfect, you're absolutely perfect!'

I smiled and introduced myself. I couldn't help but ask why she had chosen a donkey to promote the theatre. She simply said, 'Because everybody loves a donkey.' Of course I had to agree, but I wasn't so sure what the people of Henley-on-Thames would make of us – I mean, it's quite a posh place! I was confident that Pollyanne would behave herself as we paraded the streets, but I thought we'd probably be on the receiving end of some snooty stares.

A man appeared carrying a hoarding board on straps that would fit over Pollyanne's back. The board was promoting the theatre's upcoming plays. He handed one side to me and together we put it on her. It wasn't heavy and Pollyanne didn't even bother turning her head to see what was going on. Once I'd been given instructions on the route, we were ready to go. The theatre staff were commenting on how well behaved Pollyanne was and I was boasting about her good nature, when – I don't know why – my sweet and gentle donkey decided to remind me who was boss. When it was time to go, Pollyanne let out an alarmingly loud *hee-haw* and dug her hooves in. She wouldn't budge! And to make matters worse, she was blocking the door to the theatre – I was on the street at her tail end; the two theatre folk were inside at the head end. And no amount of pushing by them or pulling by me would make her move. I felt like such a fool and I could sense that my two new theatrical friends were quickly losing patience. A donkey's rear end sticking out of their front door was probably not the PR they were hoping for! In the end, I gave her a little tap on the rear and she trotted forward into the theatre's lobby, where she turned a full circle and headed back towards the door – this time facing the right way. The man sitting behind the box office desk didn't half look surprised! Pollyanne looked at the three of us with what I could swear was a cheeky grin, as if to say, 'I'm in charge around here, all right? Leave it to me and it'll all work out.' We all sighed with relief and started to giggle; maybe this wouldn't be such a disaster after all.

The next three hours whizzed by. I lost count of the people who came up to Pollyanne – old and young alike, people wearing their finest clothes and people wearing paint-splattered jeans. Pollyanne seemed to enjoy it even more than the steam rally, if that was possible. She trotted along so well and would stop alongside any children she saw for a stroke. People asked for photos and Pollyanne revelled in the attention. She was as good as gold, and there was no more naughty behaviour. I did have to keep a close eye on her whenever anyone approached with an ice cream – she has a wicked sweet tooth and I knew that she'd soon be gobbling them all up if I didn't watch out.

By the time we got back to the theatre my feet were killing me and we had a trail of people following Pollyanne. She was like the Pied Piper, leading the way. The woman from earlier came outside to thank us for everything we'd done and was delighted to see so many people asking if they could book tickets. Pollyanne stood there regally as they thanked her, looking quite at home in the opulent lobby she'd decided to explore earlier. As we made our way back to the lorry, I gave her a stroke. 'Well done, girl. You gave me a fright there to begin with, but you've been a real star today. And I think you took quite a shine to that theatre!'

News of Pollyanne's kind nature soon spread far and wide. The phone was ringing more and more with people requesting her presence at events. Queen, Sophie and the other donkeys we had previously used for fêtes and other work still received special requests too, but Pollyanne was the most popular. Sometimes I had to decline because she couldn't spend all her time on the road – she needed to be a normal donkey and have fun in the paddock with her friends.

We are always in demand around Easter, from Palm Sunday at the start of holy week through to Easter Sunday. Lots of work for donkeys! It was on Palm Sunday that Jesus rode into Jerusalem as king – on a donkey of course. When I received a call about the annual Palm Sunday parade, I was keen for Pollyanne to take part.

The Palm Sunday parade involves hundreds of people from the local community joining together to walk through the streets, celebrating by singing hymns, praying and reading from the bible. Each year, the procession is headed up by one of our donkeys. Usually we use Queen but she'd already had two primary-school bookings that week. Queen loves doing school visits so much but the parade on top of that would exhaust her. Gaggy asked who would take her place and Linda started listing possible replacements. Sophie, Charlie, Jack ... but I cut her off.

'I'm taking Pollyanne.'

'Are you sure she's ready?' Linda asked. 'It's a big step up. She's used to there being five or so people around her at a time, not a hundred odd.'

'I'm sure,' I replied. 'She's more than ready.'

I understood Linda and Gaggy's reluctance because Pollyanne would be representing the sanctuary and if she decided to be stubborn and refused to walk (and she had form!) we would be a laughing stock. There were also safety concerns. She would be walking down a road with cars slowly passing her, and if she got spooked she could end up running into the path of a car or making a bolt for it. I really didn't want to have to chase her down the lane like a lunatic! But in spite of their concerns, I had faith in my Pollyanne. I knew she could do it – I'd never met another donkey so fond of the spotlight.

*

Palm Sunday. I stood in my best clothes at the meeting point. Pollyanne had been groomed the day before by Linda: her coat was as smooth as velvet and her hooves were sparkling. Today, she would be leading the way through the streets, escorted at the head of the convoy by myself and clergy from all the nearby churches. Behind would be the combined congregations from the twelve churches taking part and then sundry visitors who, like me, saved their churchgoing for Easter and Christmas.

Everyone gathered outside Trinity Church at Charlton just before 9.30 a.m. After a short prayer we set off. Pollyanne hadn't done much walking on the road before, but she trotted along with confidence and at a good pace – not too fast and not too slow. Behind us, people started singing hymns. I was concentrating on leading Pollyanne – I didn't want to get distracted and end up taking us the wrong way. Along the route were lots of faces I recognised from the village, and others who were sanctuary regulars, amongst a sea of faces I had never seen before. There were mums with buggies, children dressed in their Sunday best, men dressed in suits, others in T-shirts and jeans, old ladies on sticks – a right mix. Everyone was smiling and singing, happy to be at such a wonderful celebration.

Twenty members of the Wantage brass band joined the procession. I was worried the loud noise would bother Pollyanne but, as ever, she took it in her stride. Then I remembered she had enjoyed a band during her outing at the steam rally and it seemed to me now that the louder the music got the more she enjoyed it. I could almost swear she had timed her footsteps to match the beat of the drum! From the corner of my eye I could see there were a couple of chaps playing cornets, another couple playing trombones. I could hear the deep tones of the tuba, the beating of the drum and the clash of the symbols as they performed 'Hosanna'. If anyone in the nearby houses had been hoping to have a Sunday morning lie-in, they were going to miffed to say the least.

When we reached the Catholic church, some members of the procession said goodbye and went inside to have their Palm Sunday service. The rest of us carried on into Wantage to the main parish church of Saint Peter and Saint Paul. The whole journey – about a mile long – took about half an hour to walk, with people stopping their cars to have a look at what was going on. The children in the procession loved waving their palm leaves and it seemed that everyone enjoyed the whole atmosphere of coming together to celebrate.

At church, the vicar stepped to one side and let Pollyanne lead everyone into the church building. We walked right down the side aisle and stood at the front, while people filed into the pews behind us. The vicar welcomed everybody and the service began. Pollyanne stood as good as gold, not moving a muscle. The Sunday school children rushed past to act out a short play, but she didn't react. She was close enough to the beautiful flower arrangements to lean over and take a nibble, but she resisted the temptation. Barron, Spike and Arthur wouldn't have had such self-control: they'd have swallowed a mouthful of carnations and forget-me-nots before I'd had a chance to stop them! She could have knocked them over with one shake of her head – I could just imagine the sound of the metal flower stand hitting the stone floor, scaring the younger children, causing childish tears and dirty looks from angry pensioners ... But Pollyanne was absolutely brilliant, as if she'd been in church all her life. When the service finished she was given the nod and we made our way outside.

'Excuse me, can I stroke her?' an eager little boy asked me, having run out the church as fast as he could behind me.

'Of course, as long as it's okay with your mum,' I replied, as a flustered woman appeared. She nodded her head and the boy reached up and stroked Pollyanne's side.

'She's beautiful,' he said, in awe of her. Pollyanne took one look at him and then glanced back at me. 'Can I have one, Mum?' he asked in all seriousness.

'No, Jonathan, you can't,' she said, firmly.

I explained to the little boy that Pollyanne had to live with her donkey friends at Island Farm Donkey Sanctuary but that he was always welcome to pop along and see her on a weekend. By the time I finished speaking quite a crowd of children had gathered and they were all eager to stroke her. Once they'd all had a turn, the older members of the congregation stepped in, wanting to stroke her too. I always find that there's something about being around animals that brings out even the most grown-up people's childish side!

After thanking the vicar for a lovely service I decided it was time to head back, as we had to walk back along the way we had come to get back to the lorry. It was a nice day so I didn't mind the walk, and it was ever so peaceful which made a nice change after all the hulla-baloo of the parade.

'Well done, Pollyanne,' I said as I patted her side. She seemed to nod and nuzzled into me. If she'd been a cat, I'm sure she would have purred. All the kicking we had to put up with in the beginning was long forgotten, Pollyanne just couldn't do enough. She was paying us back for believing in her.

After stopping for a minute or two to give her a well-deserved stroke, I told her it was time to get going so she could be back in time to go in the paddock for a run around before dinner. I felt in my pocket for my packet of mints and after popping one mint in my mouth I held one out for her. She took it and in a fraction of a second she had gulped it down. She does love a mint, our Pollyanne!

As I popped the sweets back into my pocket, I felt the brown envelope that the procession organiser had passed to me earlier. Inside were a couple of crisp notes, a little thank-you for taking part. I never charge people for events we attend, I just ask for a donation, and this usually results in people being more than generous. I couldn't wait to get back to the sanctuary to tell the others how the day had gone. I had some good news to tell Stuart too: five people had said they would be contacting him to see about adopting Pollyanne.

Money has always been a big issue for the sanctuary and it has kept me up many nights over the years. We rely completely on donations, sponsorships and on the small amounts we receive when our donkeys take part in events. It costs £10,000 a month to feed and keep the donkeys, and drumming up that kind of money is not an easy feat. That said, we would never make a donkey do an event they will not enjoy or that puts them at risk. We also select only a handful of the eighty-plus donkeys we have at the sanctuary to take part in events, those that are most suited and are the most friendly towards humans. So, much of our money has to come from adoption – for £15 a year, the adopter gets regular updates about the donkey they have chosen to support, as well as a lovely photograph. Although taking part in events like today's procession is always good fun and a nice day out for the donkey involved, it's also a crucial way of bringing attention to the work we do and – hopefully – find a few more supporters amongst the crowds.

5

Soulmates

A couple of days after the Palm Sunday event I got an emergency call late at night to see if I would take in a donkey and her foal. They had originally been cared for by a couple who had been good and responsible owners. But when the wife died, the husband sadly suffered from a mental breakdown. The donkeys had been neglected for months and were in a very bad state. A neighbour – the man on the phone – realised something had to be done. He knew the donkeys would end up

dying if he didn't act. The owner wasn't being deliber-
ately cruel, but he clearly was in no position to look after
the animals. I explained that I would need a letter from
their owner agreeing to hand over responsibility for their
care to me. We arranged to meet at 6.30 a.m. for a hand-
over. I hung up the phone, set my alarm clock for 5 a.m.,
left a note for Gaggy and Linda so they would know
where I was, and went to bed.

It was raining when I arrived, the clouds in the sky
were black and it felt like it could thunder at any
moment. Donkeys hate thunder, so I wanted to make
sure the donkey and her foal were safely loaded before
it started. The man greeted me with a handshake and
said how glad he was that I was going to look after the
animals from now on. He handed me the signed piece
of paper and I folded it up, placing it in my coat pocket.
Many people think that I have the authority to take any
donkey that is suffering but that really isn't the case. If
I took a donkey without permission I could be arrested
for stealing. If they won't sign over the donkey to me,

then I have to inform the RSPCA and let them take over.

Loading them wasn't too difficult and two hours later I arrived back at the sanctuary. There wasn't an ounce of fat on the poor mother. She was just skin and bone, like Jack had been when he arrived all those years ago. Her little foal was pressed up against her flank. They were both shaking like mad, traumatised from the long journey they had just undertaken.

'Come on, darling,' I said as I reached in and took hold of the collar she was wearing around her neck. It was well worn and stained; she must have worn it for months, if not years. I had been able to tell the second I clapped eyes on her that she wasn't a kicker – all the fight had gone from her. The little one refused to look up at me, staring instead at his mum. He followed silently as I led her out. Gaggy had appeared out of the office, thinking I might need help, but I waved him away – she wasn't going to be any trouble.

The weather had been awful all morning so there was

no point in me letting her into the rehabilitation paddock, as she'd only get wet. I led them both into a stable,
which Linda had only finished mucking out minutes
before. I put a handful of mix into a bowl in the corner,
and checked that the water trough had been topped up.
Their coats were extremely dirty and matted but I was
going to let them settle in before I cleaned them up. The
little one darted when I tried to touch him and ran
around to the far side of his mum, out of my reach. He'd
probably never been in contact with a human before, so
it was going to take time to win him round.

I said my goodbyes and then locked the stable door
behind me, just leaving the top section open so we could
duck our heads over later to check on them. I had to
hurry and get changed as Pollyanne, Queen, Linda and
myself had an appointment at Gloucester Cathedral and
if I wasn't careful we were going to be late. Pollyanne
had proved at the Palm Sunday parade that she was a
star, so I'd decided to give her an even bigger job – the
Festival of the Donkey.

103

The Festival of the Donkey is run each year by the special-needs charity Hop, Skip and Jump. Over four hundred disabled children take part, with the children who can't walk riding the donkeys. Pollyanne and Queen weren't the only animals taking part: there were six other donkeys, a goat and a dog. I was really excited as I walked up to the cathedral, so imposing that it dwarfed the people gathered around the entrance. Together we all walked round to the side entrance and were introduced to the children who would be riding Pollyanne and Queen in the performance.

Pollyanne's rider was a little girl called Toni, who had never been on a donkey before. She was a bit nervous at first but once she'd given Pollyanne a tentative stroke, I handed her a gingernut biscuit and explained that they were Pollyanne's favourite. Toni giggled, they were her favourite too. With the help of Toni's mum I lifted her onto Pollyanne's back and we had a dummy run so she could get used to the way Pollyanne moves when she walks.

When the performance was about to start all the

children and donkeys lined up ready. The children had been practising for weeks so were eager to show their families sitting inside the cathedral what they could do. As the reverend leading the service told the audience the Gospel story, the children appeared dressed as Mary and Joseph, then later John the Baptist, the disciples, the blind man who was healed and so on. It was a wonderful spectacle and I was very proud of both Pollyanne and Queen e as we led them down the aisle of the church, both with small children clinging excitedly to their backs. I could tell Pollyanne really enjoyed herself – she was lapping up the attention and seemed to be intent on making sure Toni had the time of her life. In fact, Toni had such a good time that we had a real job trying to get her off. Eventually we convinced her it was time for Pollyanne to go home for her dinner, and so she reluctantly allowed us to carefully lift her back into her wheelchair.

I was exhausted by the time we got back to the sanctuary. The early start and all the Easter events were beginning to catch up with me. I decided that I could do with an early night, and Linda and Gaggy said they'd bring the donkeys in from the stables and give them their dinner, so I could knock off for the day.

'I'll just pop in on the new arrivals before I turn in . . .' I said, casually.

As soon as the words were out of my mouth, Linda strated to laugh. She knows me almost as well as I know myself, and she knew there would be no way I would go to bed without checking them. I wouldn't be able to sleep without knowing they were okay.

As I peered over the stable door, I was glad to see that the mix I had left earlier had been eaten up. I was going to be feeding the mother small amounts at regular periods over the next few days because it was clear from the state of her that she hadn't been used to eating a lot, and the last thing I wanted was for her to get ill. Her son was too busy drinking from her to notice that I was watching them. Donkeys have two teats and feed their foals for approximately six months before they start to eat grass, straw and mix. This little fella was about four months old, maybe five, so he wouldn't be having his mother's milk for that much longer.

The next morning I woke up feeling refreshed – a few extra hours in bed had made all the difference. The rain from the day before had passed, the sky had cleared, and I could tell it was going to be a sunny spring day. After doing my usual chores, settling all the donkeys in their various paddocks, I went and got our new additions. It was time for them to be cleaned up.

The mother donkey looked very similar to Pollyanne. I hadn't really noticed before but once I had washed her coat the resemblance was clear. They could almost be twins. This new donkey was slighter than Pollyanne but from a distance it would be very difficult to tell them apart. Stuart came over, carrying a cup of tea for me, and asked me her story. I told him what I knew. It seemed to me that the mother had survived on nothing but the scant grass in her muddy paddock. Her foal had been able to survive on his mother's milk. Together they had tried to shelter under a tree whenever it rained. I didn't think they would have lived for much longer.

Both mother and foul stood patiently while I cleaned them up. Thankfully neither seemed to have any wounds or sores – they were thin and dirty, but they didn't have any more serious injuries. Still, I'd get the vet to give them a once-over next time he visited. They both looked much better once they'd had the muck cleaned off them, although neither would be winning any beauty contests for a while.

We try to come up with names for new arrivals as soon as possible to make things easier for us all – we couldn't call them 'thingy' or 'the new one' for very long. It's also nice to mark the beginning of the donkey's fresh start – to mark the new life with a new name. But these days, with over eighty donkeys, coming up with unique names isn't easy. After a bit of discussion, we decided to call the mother Tracy which means 'warlike', because we wanted her to fight and get well again. We picked Louis (Lou for short) for her son.

Sometimes when we get a donkey in, the children who visit the sanctuary help name him or her. We give them a few names to choose from, they let us know which name they like and then the most popular one wins. Diana was one such donkey. She was born here on 1 September 1997, the day after Princess Diana's death, so everyone thought the name was fitting.

One donkey was known for days after he arrived at the sanctuary as 'the donkey from Newbury'. In the end the name Newbury stuck! Mr Crusty is one of our more unusually named inhabitants, named in honour of the good people at Mr Crusty Bakery in Wallingford – they give us their leftover bread each day to bulk out the donkeys' mix.

Tracy and Lou soon settled in and before long were ready to go out in the paddock with the others. Lou had been a tricky one to win over – he wasn't at all sure of us and stuck to his mother's side like glue. Tracy could remember a time when she'd been well looked after; she remembered a time when humans had been good to her. Lou had only known neglect and the harsh conditions he'd been born into. He had no reason to trust anyone but his mother. But with lots of patience, he slowly learned to trust us and come out of his shell and by the time we were ready to introduce the pair to the rest of the gang, he was much more confident. Within days he had turned into a cheeky little thing, running about and causing mischief wherever he could. He tried to get the grown-ups to play chase with him but they were always more interested in grazing. It made me smile to watch him dart about the older donkeys; he seemed to be saying, 'Play with me! Play with me!' and the grown-ups would sigh, 'Not now, little one.' Lou was never put off, though – he kept trying, bless him.

When Lou was fully weaned and no longer dependent on Tracy, we moved him into the boys' paddock. Luckily for Lou, there were some young boys in the group that wouldn't mind joining in with his running games. Tracy did pine for him for a day or two, but we gave her lots of love and attention and she was soon back to her old self.

'Are you nearly ready? They'll be here any minute,' I called out to Linda who was in our largest barn, sorting out the riding helmets. Pollyanne, Tracy, Chocolate, Queen and Diana were in the yard, wearing their saddles. Well, Pollyanne was ready and waiting patiently ... the others were giving me a headache. Every time I got them all standing still, I'd turn my back for a moment and one would wander off.

The group had all been picked out for the riding day because of their good temperaments, their easy way with children and their size – not too big, not too small. Tracy had been at the sanctuary for nearly six months now, and was unrecognisable from the donkey I first met that thundery day. I had put her in the line in between Queen and Diana, but she had decided she wanted to stand beside Pollyanne. In the end I let her do what she wanted – trying to control five donkeys with minds of their own was more trouble than it was worth! She snuggled in next to Pollyanne, who turned and rested her head on Tracy's shoulder. Seeing them together was a bit eerie, they were so alike.

I heard the children outside, chattering away excitedly, and pulled open the barn doors. Rory, Rachel, Rebecca, Chloe and Frankie had arrived with their parents for their weekly riding lesson. I am a firm believer in children learning how to ride – it gives them confidence, a sense of responsibility and gets them out in the fresh air. The donkeys love it, too. We tend to give lessons to littler children who aren't quite ready for ponies.

'Come on then, Rory, you can ride Pollyanne today,' I said to a blond boy as I passed him his helmet and gave him a leg up. Rachel was on Tracy, Rebecca rode Chocolate, Chloe and Queen made another pair and Frankie was on Diana. To begin with, I start the donkeys walking round clockwise, then anti-clockwise while instructing the children all about the basics of riding. Some of the children struggle to concentrate but it doesn't really matter, the donkeys lead the way. After about fifteen minutes we set off for a slow walk around the sanctuary.

Pollyanne led the way, with Tracy closely following behind her. They were so alike in temperament, so gentle, kind and loving. We hacked out into the fields so the children could just enjoy being outdoors with the donkeys. Before the lesson finished I got them to dismount and then walk with me around the edge of the paddock so I could point out the different birds, plants and flowers. Sometimes children today are so preoccupied by TV, or with playing their X-Box, that they don't see how beautiful nature is.

I get so much enjoyment from teaching these children to ride – to see the joy on their faces makes everything worthwhile. The donkeys enjoy it too, and I like to think that when their saddles are off and they are back in the paddock, they brag to the others, 'Guess where I've been?'

When the lesson was over and the children had handed me their helmets, they all skipped off to their parents. Rory was the last to go, telling his mum, 'I love Pollyanne, she's the best.'

As Linda and I led the donkeys back to the barn to take their saddles off, I mentioned how Tracy seemed to become Pollyanne's shadow.

'I've noticed too,' she said. 'I think maybe they've met their match!'

Over the next few weeks, I noticed that Pollyanne was not following me around as much as she used to. Now she followed Tracy. When it was time to come in from the fields, they would walk side by side, and each morning when they saw each other again they would rub muzzles in greeting. I was so happy to see that they had bonded – they had both had such hard starts in life, and were both such sweet-natured things – that I wanted them to know the companionship that is so important to donkeys. I suggested to Linda that the next time Pollyanne had a church event or school outing, Tracy should go along and learn the ropes. Maybe eventually she could stand in for Pollyanne from time to time. Linda agreed that it made perfect sense – and that it would prevent Tracy from pining for Pollyanne if she was left alone at the sanctuary for a day.

My favourite donkey had found her soulmate!

6

An Agent Calls

I had been preparing the mix for the donkey's evening meal over by the barn when I saw Stuart waving at me from the office, shouting something that I couldn't make out from that distance. I carried on cutting the bread into chunks and slicing the carrots, mixing everything well in with the grains so that the mix was even and one donkey wouldn't end up with a dinner of mostly carrots while another one had none.

I had just finished filling the feeding trolley when

Linda appeared. 'You're needed in the office,' she said. 'Stuart's got something urgent he needs to tell you.'

'Can't it wait? I'm running late as it is, it'll be going dark soon.'

'Don't worry, I'll take over while you're gone, you'll be back in a couple of minutes.'

'Okay, okay,' I said, wondering what on earth could be so urgent. I was halfway across the yard when Stuart opened the office door and shouted, 'Hurry up, Dad!' I looked at him, and could see that he was smiling from ear to ear. Whatever he was going to tell me, it had to be good news.

I scraped the mud off my shoes at the door and stepped inside the office. The heat hit me instantly – I'd been working in the cold all day and I immediately started shedding layers. Stuart and Wendy were both sitting there with ridiculous grins on their faces. I couldn't begin to imagine what had made them so happy.

'Have we won the lottery?' I asked, hoping that might be true.

Wendy opened her mouth to answer, but before she could say a word, Stuart burst out: 'Pollyanne's going to be famous!'

'What are you going on about?' Had I heard him right?

Wendy explained. 'I've just had a lady on the phone. That's why we called you in. She's an agent specialising in animal performers. She wants to represent Pollyanne!'

'But she's a *donkey*! Why on earth does she need an agent?'

'She thinks Pollyanne could be in TV shows, adverts, all sorts. Pollyanne the actress . . . what do you think?'

'I think we need to think about it.' I knew she could do it, Pollyanne excelled in whatever task I gave her, but I needed to find out more. We'd had our brief brushes with show-business in the past, but this sounded like a much bigger deal. Pollyanne with an agent? It sounded bonkers to me.

'She's going to send through the details for you to look at.' Wendy smiled. 'Even if she doesn't do it, it's nice that they thought of us.'

Pollyanne – the undisputed star of Island Farm Donkey Sanctuary
© Hannah Boursnell

The donkeys of Island Farm grazing in the paddocks.

Countess, Diana and Duchess.

Monty and Mr Crusty.

Queen, Mrs P and Pollyanne.

Pollyanne and Linda at St Teresa's Catholic Church
Palm Sunday celebrations.

Travelling in style.

Pollyanne is mobbed by her fans!

Outside the Royal Opera House – a long way from Island Farm!

The view from the stage of the Royal Opera House. Red velvet seats as far as the eye can see . . .

Ildebrando D'Arcangelo riding Pollyanne's pal, Louis, with Anna Caterina Antonacci and the cast of *Carmen*.

It'll be all right on the night . . . John and Pollyanne on stage with the cast of Carmen.

© Catherine Ashmore

Peace and quiet! Pollyanne back home with her friends at the Island Farm Donkey Sanctuary.

An Agent Calls

A few days later I got to speak to the agent and we talked at length. Her name was Kay Weston and she was from an agency called Animal Ambassadors. She had seen Pollyanne and a few of our other donkeys at an event, and been struck by how eager Pollyanne was, how much she enjoyed attention and how giving she was to the people who came to see her.

Kay had been working with animals for over fifteen years and she had a whole host of different creatures on her books. TV companies, journalists, theatres and other people involved in show-business would ring her up whenever they needed a particular animal for a project, and she would sort them out.

As it turned out, Kay had a specific job in mind for Pollyanne. An opera. What had seemed incredible to begin with now seemed completely unbelievable. A donkey in an opera? Granted, I'd never been to the opera, but I imagined a stage packed with big fat singers, all screeching away. Not a little donkey hee-hawing the house down. And it got more far-fetched the more I found out: the opera in question was to be staged at the Royal Opera House in Covent Garden. I had thought maybe it would be little local theatre, like the one we'd visited in Henley. But no, it was one of the most prestigious opera houses in the world. And its star was none other than Plácido Domingo, surely one of the most famous tenors in the world. Even I'd heard of him!

Pollyanne would be performing two or three times a week for one month. On top of that, she would have to rehearse for a couple of weeks in advance of the opening night. I was pleased it wouldn't be every day because I didn't want to disrupt Pollyanne's routine too much. I still wanted her to be a normal donkey.

I wanted to meet Kay face to face before agreeing to anything so she made the trip up to see us. She arrived wearing worn jeans, a waterproof and green wellies . . . and even though it was chucking it down she was happy to walk in the thick mud to the stables. She was really down to earth and lovely, and you could tell just by looking at her when she was stroking and talking to the donkeys that she was a big animal lover. I immediately felt much better about the whole thing.

I was a bit nervous introducing her to Pollyanne in case she wasn't what Kay was looking for. I needn't have worried, though, because Kay said she was perfect and took photos from every angle to send on to the Royal Opera House, if I was happy to proceed. She explained that she would also keep some photos on file in case another theatre or TV company contacted her in the future to ask if she had a donkey available.

Kay explained how Animal Ambassadors always put the animal's welfare first and insisted on maintaining a healthy and safe environment for the animals to work in, which reassured me a great deal. She also explained in detail how great the Royal Opera House is when it comes to looking after the animals that work on its stage. It turns out animals appear in operas all the time. Well, you learn something new every day! Kay had supplied two cob horses called Jack and Jill for their staging of the opera *Katya Kabanova*; for *The Magic Flute* she had supplied a peregrine falcon and for Donizetti's *L'elisir d'amore* she had provided Ozzie, a Jack Russell terrier. She knew the casting director and crew well and was quick to assure me Pollyanne would be treated like a princess during her time there.

After hearing this I decided it was time I introduced Kay to Linda, Gaggy, Stuart and Wendy as it was important that they got to know her. I could only agree for Pollyanne to be on Kay's books and appear in the opera if the whole team were behind me, as they would have to hold the fort on performance days. While Kay nipped to her car to pick up the paperwork she needed, we had a whispered conference about it all. I told them Kay seemed really trustworthy and they immediately agreed we should go for it. When Stuart reminded me that the fee would pay our water, gas and electricity bills for the year, and that we would be able to replace our broken trailer, the decision was as good as made.

I'm not sure whether Kay could sense that we'd all been talking about her when she stepped back inside the office but she smiled and handed me the contract. I took a pen from the desk and signed my name, on behalf of Pollyanne of course. She was officially going to be a West End star!

The opera Pollyanne would be appearing in was called *I Pagliacci*. I didn't know anything about it back then, but now I could chat about it happily for hours. It's by an Italian composer called Leoncavallo and, like a lot of operas, it's tragic love story. When the morning of the first rehearsal came around, I still wasn't sure what Pollyanne's role in the story could possibly be, but I was eager to find out.

I had been tossing and turning all the night before, thinking everything over. In the end I gave up on sleep and got up, even though it was only 4.30 a.m. I decided to get the morning chores out of the way and take my mind off the day ahead.

Kay arrived just after 7 a.m. She was going to be travelling with us in the lorry so had decided to meet us here rather than us picking her up en route in case it unsettled Pollyanne. I wanted to make sure her big day was as stress-free as possible.Pollyanne was bright eyed when we went into her stable and didn't object when I put on her head collar. Linda had groomed her the day before and she still looked immaculate. We might have only been going to a rehearsal but I wanted her to make a good first impression – I certainly wouldn't want to turn up with her covered in dust and dirt from the paddock. Tracy tried to follow us out, but I had to tell her that she was staying behind this time. She did look forlorn, poor thing.

On the road, Kay kept me amused with her stories of things that had happened on photo shoots and TV shows. She had had lots of funny experiences – you know what they say: never work with children or animals! I could only hope that Pollyanne would maintain her immaculate track record and not get up to any mischief today.

Travelling from the sanctuary to the theatre didn't take

too long, but the change in scenery was remarkable. From the little twisty lanes near the sanctuary, surrounded by nothing but open fields and pretty villages, to wide, bustling streets with towering buildings on every side. From green to grey. Driving the lorry was tricky – the cars in front kept changing lanes and there were more buses than I'd seen in my life. I wasn't exactly sure where to go, and although Kay tried to direct me in good time I kept missing the turns because people wouldn't let me in. The thought of doing this journey a couple of times a week for several months was daunting, to say the least. By the time we arrived at the theatre I felt like I'd aged twenty years! I wished I'd had more sleep as I felt absolutely exhausted and we'd barely begun the day. Oh well, I'd just have to have a cup of tea and buck up. Pollyanne needed me to be on top form today.

I parked up on Floral Street, as close to the Royal Opera House as we could get. Kay placed a special badge on the dashboard to tell any passing traffic wardens that we had permission to be there. If I'd have been in the lorry on my own I'd have probably taken a few minutes to compose myself – I was totally out of my comfort zone. I closed my eyes for one second and heard Kay open the passenger side door and jump out. 'Come on, John,' she said, smiling at me. 'There's nothing to worry about.'

I jumped out of the lorry and had a quick look around. I must admit, my impression of London so far hadn't been great, but Covent Garden looked completely different. It was like an old town square, with cobbled streets and a pillared market building in the centre. Not what I had expected at all. Kay helped me unload Pollyanne and then the three of us made our way to the Royal Opera House. The sight of that building for the very first time took my breath away. The front of the building – a magnificent classical edifice with six impressive Roman-style columns – was constructed in 1858 but the rest of the building was completely redesigned in the nineties and is more modern. As Kay told me a little bit about its history, I glanced round at the people walking past, wearing all kinds of fashions, speaking many different languages, bustling hither and thither. It was nothing like Brightwell-cum-Sotwell, that's for sure. I wondered what they made of the old country bumpkin and his grey donkey . . .

Kay led us round the corner to the stage door. Next to it was another, very tall, door, which Kay told me was designed to allow large pieces of scenery or animals into the theatre. Apparently it's called the Giraffe Door! She used the buzzer to announce our arrival and the door opened. Kay had been to the Opera House so many times that she knew exactly where to go, which made me feel better. I followed behind with Pollyanne close by my side. I think we each made the other feel less on edge. We reached the stage via a lift and I saw that there were about twenty people standing about with scripts. Kay introduced me to Emily Gottlieb, the stage manager. She seemed to be in charge and was delighted to meet Pollyanne, having heard all about her from Kay. She took us backstage where they had constructed a pen for

Pollyanne to wait in before and after her time on stage and then explained exactly what Pollyanne would be required to do. She walked me through the whole thing and gave me a piece of paper that explained exactly when Pollyanne should be on stage so that I could try to learn it. She was very patient and calm and I immediately started to relax.

The stage was massive – a sea of black stretching for what seemed like miles before it reached the orchestra pit. I'd been imagining something a lot smaller and was relieved that there would be little danger of Pollyanne toppling over the edge. The crew were busy fixing the set together: huge buildings and rock structures – double the height of normal houses and twice as wide – built over three levels. It took eight men to move each of the various sections, even though they were on wheels. Ladders were placed behind the structures and Emily told me that when the cast stood on them, it would appear to the audience that they were standing on top of the walls and buildings that made up the set. One chap climbed nimbly up a ladder with a guitar-like instrument strapped to his back and then started playing it once he reached the top. I don't know how he managed to balance – I'd have fallen off and broken my leg if I'd tried it.

Emily explained that *Pagliacci* is about a love triangle between three clowns from a touring troupe who are putting on a play. Canio is the leader and is married to Nedda and they are joined by fellow clowns Beppe and Tonio. I tried to concentrate as Emily explained the very complicated plot to me, making a mental note to ask Stuart or Neil to find out the story and write it all down for me when I got home so I could learn it. Not that I expected to be tested on my opera knowledge or anything, but I thought it would be better to be safe than sorry.

The cast had been rehearsing for a long time but Pollyanne had only been brought in for the last few rehearsals. I kept getting in the way of everyone, as it seemed everyone was in a rush to get ready before the first run-through. There was a lot of shouting going on, but I couldn't understand what was being said as it was all in Italian or Spanish. Kay gave me a reassuring squeeze on my arm and whispered that it'd be fine. I was to do the run-through with Pollyanne and then after a couple of goes one of the actresses was going to take over from me, so I could sit in the audience and watch.

All of a sudden, the chatter died down and Emily told me it was time for the first run-through of the day. We had to get off stage, quick sharp. I walked Pollyanne into her pen and stayed with her there, trying to calm my nerves. Then all of a sudden, the orchestra started up. This was it. I had never seen an opera before and I hadn't expected the music to make the hairs on the back of my neck stand up but they did. We were on the right-hand side of the stage and I couldn't see very much, but I could hear every word. Even though it was in a different language, I found it very emotional. Gaggy would have said I was going soft if he'd been there.

The cast weren't wearing their costumes so it was hard to make out who was cast and who was crew. People kept walking past us, holding an assortment of props and chattering away, but Pollyanne wasn't bothered at all. She just stood there quietly as if this was all normal to her. When it was finally our turn, Emily came and gave us a nod and so I knew that it was time for us to stand in position.

As I stood in the wings with Pollyanne I told myself I was silly to feel nervous – there was no audience watching, after all. I took a deep breath and stepped tentatively into the bright lights of the stage. For a moment I stood completely still, frozen to the spot, but then Pollyanne pulled forward and I went with her, following the cast members in front of us. We were at the top of three levels, in a procession line, and were making our way down ramps to the lower level. I was still feeling very nervous and was finding it hard to remember how to put one foot in front of another. But every time I faltered, Pollyanne gave a little tug on her rope to remind me to keep up and I set off again. The set was very bright and colourful and acrobats were tumbling all around us. The heat from the lights was intense and the music almost overpowering; I got lost in the moment. I felt like we could have almost been in Italy, so I was surprised when we reached the lower level and I looked out and saw rows and rows of red velvet chairs as far as the eye could see. A fire eater went past, attempting to swallow flames from a burning stick he was holding. The procession came to a halt and a man hung from the side of it beating a huge drum to silence everyone. Plácido Domingo, playing Canio, spoke to the gathered crowd, telling them that the play was going to start an hour before sunset.

Plácido is a huge opera star and according to Kay the whole cast were excited to have the opportunity to work with him. He has a reputation as one of the greatest ever opera singers and had performed many times alongside Luciano Pavarotti and José Carreras as one of the famous Three Tenors. He was the best of the best ... and

Pollyanne was going to be sharing a stage with him. Incredible.

When 'Canio' had finished singing, he threw some sweets at the crowd who had gathered on stage to hear him. One sweet fell ever so close to Pollyanne and I tightened my grip on her rope, but she just ignored it. I know that if I'd been on stage with any of the other donkeys from the sanctuary, that sweet would have disappeared faster than you could blink.

After about five minutes one of the actors gave me a wink, which was my signal to take Pollyanne over to the other side of the stage. I had started to enjoy myself by this point, and as walked around the crowds, I felt like applauding the amazing acrobats who were tumbling all around us. As instructed, we stopped centre-stage alongside Plácido Domingo. He leant forward and placed colourful garlands around Pollyanne's neck. Without prompting, she bowed her head as if receiving a medal and then looked up, facing the auditorium. I tugged gently on her rope to indicate that it was time to leave the stage but she stood there for a moment longer, seeming to gaze out over an imaginary audience. Then she turned smartly and trotted off stage-right. (I might have only been 'in the theatre' for an hour but I had already picked up the lingo. What a luvvie!)

Once we were back safely in the wings I exhaled and lowered myself into a nearby chair. It was only now that I realised how much my poor legs were shaking. That was one of the scariest things I'd ever done – and it was simply a rehearsal. I definitely wasn't made for the stage and was just relieved that I would only be doing it for a couple more times and then an actress would be taking over and leading Pollyanne on stage.

As usual, Pollyanne had done me proud. There had been so many people dashing about all around her: acrobats, fire eaters, strange people singing very loudly. She just took it all in her stride, as if she'd been appearing on stage her whole life. As I gave her a gingernut biscuit and stroked her back to say thanks, I remembered the theatre in Henley and her naughty little trip into the lobby. Maybe *she* was the luvvie – happiest amongst the red velvet curtains and the gilded chairs of the theatre; at home with the smell of greasepaint and the roar of the crowd. Once Act I finished the rest of the cast came over and made a big fuss of her, telling her how good she was. Kay was equally pleased – she had found the perfect donkey actress.

Before Act II started the costume designer introduced herself and asked if I could follow her. I left Pollyanne in her pen with Kay watching her and followed her down a maze of corridors before we arrived in one of the costume rooms. There were literally hundreds of costumes in there on huge rails that stretched from one side of the room to the other. I didn't quite understand why she wanted me as I wasn't going to be doing any of the performances myself. Before I could ask, she disappeared behind a rack and shouted for me to take a seat. I did as I was told and perched myself on a stool by a fancy sewing machine. Her desk was covered in brightly coloured fabrics, and a half-sewn jacket which I presumed was for one of the clowns.

A couple of seconds later she reappeared, with her arms full of colourful costumes: a pink tutu, a straw hat, blue and yellow stripy trousers and a green cloak of some description. She dropped them all on her desk and handed me the hat. 'It's for Pollyanne,' she said, and as I inspected it I noticed that she'd cut two holes in the top for Pollyanne's ears. It was decorated with fake sunflowers and had streamers hanging from it. I'd never tried to put a hat on her before, but I thought she'd probably be okay with it. The only worry would be if she tried to eat the streamers as they would be dangling just inches from her face. The designer explained that the blanket hanging over a chair in the corner was for Pollyanne too. I would just need to drape it over her back before she went on stage. She reassured me that if Pollyanne hated her hat, we could always change it for something else. To be honest, I was just relieved that the pink tutu wasn't for Pollyanne – she'd never have lived it down at the sanctuary!

After a quick lunch, we ran through our part again. I was a lot more relaxed this time around and I tried my best to get into character a bit, rather than just walking around as John from the donkey sanctuary. I tried Pollyanne's hat on her and she didn't seem to mind it although getting it to stay on wasn't easy.

When it was time to go and we stepped onto the street, I couldn't get over how bright everything was. Because I'd been in the dark for hours, it took a while for my eyes to readjust. I suggested we took Pollyanne for a quick walk before heading home as she needed to stretch her legs. I was glad to be outside, as was Pollyanne, and she trotted along happily between me and Kay. There were lots of tourists about with cameras hanging from their necks and I noticed that a few of them were taking photos of Pollyanne. We walked past several open air cafés and restaurants and everyone seemed to be staring at us, like they'd never seen a donkey before. We passed a man dressed like a statue, who was standing so still that I thought he actually *was* a statue, until he pointed at Pollyanne and then at his collection cap on the floor before freezing again. We carried on walking, past a lady belting out show tunes while playing a keyboard and a magician doing card tricks. There was so much to see that I would have happily carried on walking and taking it all in, but as we paused to watch a mime artist, people started coming up to us asking if their kids could have a ride on Pollyanne, or asking us for photos, and in the end we were surrounded by nearly thirty people. I tried to make the excuse that Pollyanne needed to get back home but they wouldn't listen and in the end we had to force our way through the crowds and hurry back to Floral Street as quickly as possible. Swarmed by fans! Pollyanne was definitely on her way to becoming a superstar now!

7

Prima Donkey

Before I knew it it was the big day: opening night. The rehearsals had all gone well and I was so excited to see how it all came together when the curtain rose. Seeing all the people I'd come to know over the past few weeks in full makeup and costume was quite surreal. One of the actors came over to say hello to us and I didn't recognise him at all – it took me a good few seconds to realise it was one of the singers who'd always been particularly kind to Pollyanne. It was a tight squeeze in the wings and I don't know how we would have found Jane, who would be leading Pollyanne, unless she had sought us out.

When it was nearly time for Pollyanne to go on stage I led her out of her pen and handed her rope over to Jane. Jane gave Pollyanne a quick stroke before leading her away. Pollyanne gave a quick glance back as she walked off, as if to say, 'Aren't you coming?'

That look gave me a pang and I recognised the feeling in the pit of my stomach as the same feeling I had had many, many years ago when Stuart had started school. For the next fifteen minutes I sat in my seat next to Pollyanne's pen backstage, twiddling my thumbs, hoping that she would perform as well as she had in the rehearsals. There were two thousand people in the audience, in the final rehearsal there had only been fifty. I had no idea if seeing so many people would freak Pollyanne out – I just hoped she would enjoy herself as much as she had in rehearsals.

The second her face appeared from behind the curtain,

I knew everything was okay. I can read her face: she looked happy. I broke out into a beaming smile and rushed over to give her a cuddle. I was so proud of her. Jane said Pollyanne had performed brilliantly, as if she'd been acting on a stage all her life. I can't put into words how happy I was – I wanted to ring Stuart right away but I had to wait until the interval, it was torture having to wait. As soon as the audience's rapturous applause had died down at the end of the show, I dashed to the phone to tell everyone back home about our little star.

We soon got into the swing of travelling up and down to London for the performances. And I'm happy to say I eventually got the hang of the traffic! Pollyanne's performance continued to cause a sensation and soon we were having to deal with media requests. Can you believe it? Everyone wanted to know more about Pollyanne and the office phone was ringing constantly. We did interviews for our local newspaper, and the national press too. Journalists were keen to capture

Pollyanne in her natural habitat, so to speak, and so we had photographer after photographer turning up at the sanctuary. The other donkeys were very bemused, with a few of them trying to sneak into the photos with her! I didn't mind them taking photos of Pollyanne but each time they asked me to pose alongside her I grimaced – I don't like having my photo taken one little bit.

Wendy was the first to notice that the sanctuary was getting many more visitors than usual and when she asked people were they were from, she was finding out that they'd travelled for three, four hours to come and see the famous donkey they'd been reading about in their papers. The extra money in the donation box was certainly welcomed and many said they would be coming back again.

Before one Tuesday-night performance the whole cast and crew were gathered on stage and told that the BBC were going to be recording the show and broadcasting it on the following Saturday night. Emily reassured everyone that although it was an important night, they should all try and pretend the BBC weren't there at all. I was so glad that I wasn't the one having to lead Pollyanne around the stage, as I wouldn't have been able to do it knowing that thousands upon thousands of people were going to listen to the whole performance on their radios a few days later. I suppose it could have been worse – it could have been shown on TV. If I'd been doing it, I would have probably tripped over my feet or bumped into one of the acrobats. Thankfully it was Jane who was in charge, and she was actually *excited* about the BBC being there.

I was a nervous wreck while Pollyanne was on stage, but as usual I had no reason to worry and it all went smoothly. I put her in her pen and sat back in my seat to wait until the interval. I knew the score quite well by now and was enjoying one of Canio and Nedda's beautiful duets – the music is so overwhelming that you really can get lost in it. Then, all of a sudden: HEE HAW! HEE HAW! Pollyanne let out the biggest bray of her life.

It was so deafening – louder than the singers, I'm sure. It was as if she was trying to join in! I leapt out of my seat and raced over to her. She stopped straight away and looked at me as if butter wouldn't melt. The stage-hands started to laugh but I was mortified. I don't know what had brought it on, I just hoped it didn't get us in trouble! I couldn't believe she'd chosen this night, of all nights, to make such a racket. That dreadful noise was now preserved for posterity on a BBC recording.

When the curtain came down and the backstage area filled up with performers and crew, plenty of people came over to us to have a giggle about Pollyanne's solo. They all told me not to worry, but I was anxious about what Emily and the other people in charge would say. I didn't want to get Emily in trouble with the BBC as she'd always been so kind to us. I looked for her amongst the crowds but I couldn't see her anywhere. As I was searching, I almost ran into Plácido Domingo but did a quick about-turn before he could collar me and complain about Pollyanne's behaviour. In the end, I decided to take Pollyanne home. If they wanted to give us our marching orders, they'd just have to do it over the phone.

By the time we arrived back at the sanctuary it was pitch black and I quickly led Pollyanne into her stable and settled her in with some mix and fresh water. I wasn't in the least bit cross with her – she was just being a donkey, after all – so I gave her a quick brush down and a tickle behind the ears before I left her for the night. I wanted to make sure she knew she hadn't done anything wrong. I patted the dogs on their heads and together we walked from stable to stable, checking that every donkey was happy and their stable doors were firmly secure.

After the drama of the previous day, it was nice to wake up to a normal day at the sanctuary. I was up just before seven and then out in the paddocks by eight. I told Stuart and Wendy that the BBC had been at the previous night's performance but didn't mention anything about

Pollyanne's impromptu singalong – I wanted to know if we'd blown our chances of performing there again before I told anyone what had happened. They both said they'd be tuning in as they hadn't been able to make the trip to London to see a performance yet. I nodded, thinking they'd definitely be in for a surprise, and then headed out to fix more clips to the barn door. Mulan and Daffy had both been causing trouble and it wasn't even nine o'clock!

Mulan is our escape artiste donkey – he is a master at opening doors. It doesn't matter how firmly you bolt a stable door, he can use his teeth to slide the catch across. Once he's free he goes to the neighbouring stables to release the donkeys that live there, and then on to the next stable and so on. He's a right little revolutionary. If he had his way he'd let every donkey in the sanctuary out in the middle of the night for a bit of fun. We've added clips to the stable doors but he still manages to undo these, although we've discovered that he'll open one clip but if there's a second he'll usually leave it alone. His accomplice is Daffy who likes to break into the barn when no one's looking. We'll just be walking past and notice that the door's ajar and when we stick our heads inside we'll find Daffy, with his head in a trough full of mix or munching on some carrots. As soon as he sees us looking at him he'll stop, pause for a moment and then carry on. He knows that we're soft touches and would never punish him, so he has a few more mouthfuls and then trots back outside to tell his friends what he's been up to.

When I finished fixing the door I knew I should ring Kay and see if she'd heard anything from Emily, but instead I went to see how Pollyanne was doing. The conversation I'd been dreading could wait a little bit longer. She was at the far side of the front paddock but as soon as she saw me coming she trotted over with Tracy and Queen. It didn't take long for the others in the paddock to notice me and soon I was surrounded. They are a bit like overexcited children when they see me – they race over, push each other out the way and try to get as close to me as possible. It wouldn't be as bad if there was just four or five of them but there can be thirty donkeys in each paddock. The newest donkeys always stay at the back when I enter the paddock because they don't understand why the others are so happy to see me. All they have known of man has been bad things: beatings and cruel acts. Over time they come around and are soon trying to get to the front of the queue for a stroke and a cuddle.

Standing there in the paddock, surrounded by all the donkeys, I immediately felt so much better. They were what was important, at the end of the day. It had been so much fun to work at the Royal Opera House – a once in a lifetime experience for me and Pollyanne – but if we never went back there again, we would still have lots of wonderful memories and we'd go back to our normal life gladly. With this new confidence, I walked over to the office and found Kay's phone number. For once there was no one else in there and I was glad of it. I sat on the edge of the desk and started to dial. Then I saw that next to Kay's number there was the mobile number Emily had given me in case we needed to contact her urgently. I decided to bite the bullet and call her directly: I wanted to have the chance to apologise to her as she had been so helpful to us.

'Hello? Is that Emily? It's John, from Island Farm.'

'John! Hello. How are you? Is everything right? Is Pollyanne sick?'

Well, she certainly sounded cheerful enough, but she was bound to be in the middle of something and perhaps she didn't want to tell me the bad news until she was somewhere private. I could picture her now, standing on the stage with her phone clamped to her ear, waving a member of the crew into the right position and picking up a rogue prop from the floor all at the same time. It seemed to me that a stage manager was always doing ten things at once. I took a deep breath.

'No, no . . . Pollyanne's fine. Well, I mean she's not ill as such—' I was rambling, I knew it. 'What I mean is, I'm ringing to ask if you want us to come back?'

'Why on earth wouldn't I want you to come back?' Emily sounded incredulous.

'After last night,' I explained. 'She made such a noise during the duet – it must be on the tape and has probably ruined the recording. I'm so sorry.'

'John, it's fine. I promise you! I tried to find you after the performance last night to tell you that the producer from the BBC loved it. There's no way to let a radio audience know there's a donkey on stage unless it makes a noise. He said he wished he'd thought of it beforehand!'

I let out a huge sigh of relief.

'You're sure? We're not sacked?'

'Certainly not. Over my dead body, in fact. Pollyanne's the star of the show and we wouldn't dream of carrying on without her.'

I was so relieved! I didn't want them thinking badly of Pollyanne and to hear that they were actually pleased with what she'd done was wonderful. The show would go on after all!

*

I was so busy all weekend that by Saturday afternoon I had completely forgotten about the opera being played on the radio. It wasn't until I heard knocking at my front door at 6.25 and saw Stuart, Gaggy, Wendy and Linda queuing up outside that I remembered. Wendy had a bottle of champagne with her, even though it was still early, so that we could all toast Pollyanne's success. I let them all in and then quickly tidied up the main living area as quickly as I could. It was a bit of a squeeze but they all insisted they wanted to listen to it together. I had two minutes to spare so frantically tried to tune my radio to the right frequency, as I usually only listen to our local station. I managed it just as the announcer finished the introduction to *Pagliacci*.

While the others got comfy I went over to the kitchen cupboards to search for glasses for the champagne – not an easy task. In the end we had to make do with a couple of stripy mugs, two pint glasses and a wine glass I found at the back of the smallest cupboard. The others were concentrating on listening but I couldn't help but think about Pollyanne. In an ideal world I'd have squeezed Pollyanne and Tracy in to share the moment, but I'd just have to tell them all about it in the morning. 'Will we be able to tell when Pollyanne's on stage?' Gaggy asked, struggling to understand what the heck was going on. 'It's all double Dutch to me.'

I sat down next to him and briefly tried to explain the plot to him, remembering how confusing I'd found it all only a few months ago. I was halfway through explaining what happens in the first two scenes when I remembered that Pollyanne's outburst would be on the recording. I took a big gulp of champagne. 'Yes, you'll be able to hear Pollyanne in about fifteen minutes,' I told him, then burst out laughing. 'You'll hear her all right.'

Everyone concentrated to start with, but after a while I could tell everyone was starting to drift off – we'd finished the champagne and I'd opened a bottle of red. I didn't let them know when they would hear Pollyanne but once the duet started I put down my mug, and stared at the radio, waiting for the commotion to start. Stuart noticed I'd gone quiet and signalled for the others to stop talking and listen. Everyone simultaneously leant forward, and then we heard in the background, 'Hee haw! Hee haw!' They all burst out laughing. It was just as if Pollyanne was in the room with us after all. The singing carried on for a moment but then Stuart reached over and turned the radio off. 'No need to listen to any more of it, we've heard Pollyanne's part,' he said, with a grin on his face.

'Thank goodness for that,' Gaggy added. 'That's enough opera to last me a lifetime. No offence to Pollyanne.'

'I felt so proud when I heard her, she truly is a star,' Wendy said as she started to gather up everyone's glasses and cups. We chatted for another ten or so minutes and then everyone left. As I shut the door behind them I couldn't help but smile. Okay, Pollyanne shouldn't have hee hawed, but like Wendy I had felt proud when I heard her.

As I pulled into Floral Street the following Tuesday, the day of our next performance, I struggled to park as there were over a hundred people standing about, filling the pavement and spilling out onto the street. Normally there are only a handful of people walking by so I couldn't understand it. Maybe a celebrity was doing a public appearance or something, but I couldn't see any banners or T-shirts emblazoned with a pop star's face. After parking up, I jumped out and went to the back to unload Pollyanne, hoping I'd be able to get her through this crowd. Before I could even open the door, a woman called out, 'The donkey's here!' and the people who had been waiting rushed over, surrounding the lorry from every side. I was dumbstruck, I hadn't a clue what was going on. It was as if they were expecting the Beatles or something.

They were all clapping and cheering 'Pollyanne! Pollyanne!' over and over again.

'I don't understand why you're all here!' I said to one chap.

He just laughed. 'We heard her on the radio,' he replied, and the people gathered all around started to nod. There were pushing each other from side to side, trying to get as close to me and Pollyanne as possible. One lady near the front was wearing a jacket covered in donkey pictures and another was carrying a donkey stuffed toy. I could see loads of cameras being pointed in our direction, as well as a bag of carrots.

'I've been waiting here the longest!' one woman called out. 'Three hours I've been waiting here.' Her husband nodded – he looked just as donkey obsessed as the rest. 'We're going to see the show tonight. See her in action.'

I was scared there was going to be a riot if I didn't get Pollyanne out of the lorry but I wanted to make sure she was safe first. I told them all to stand back so I could pull the ramp down and they all did, apart from one cheeky woman who tried to dart forward. She was soon pulled back by the others who told her to wait her turn. I said they could stroke Pollyanne if they just let me get her out.

Pollyanne must have a bit surprised when I lowered the ramp to see so many faces staring at her but she didn't seem bothered at all, and trotted off the lorry without a care in the world to receive her public. Thankfully we were a good hour early so I didn't need to rush. 'She's gorgeous,' one lady in a purple mac remarked. 'Does she want a polo mint?' Another woman tried to thrust a carrot in her direction but I calmly explained that she couldn't eat anything before her performance. They seemed to understand and gradually the crowd dispersed once everyone had had a stroke and a photograph. Lots of them were going to see the performance, even the ones who had never been to see an opera before. I just hoped that they wouldn't clap and cheer when she came on stage as I didn't want us to get into even more trouble. I could imagine the newspaper headlines … 'Donkey causes chaos at Opera House', 'Plácido Domingo quits because of donkey madness'. My head started to spin.

Once inside, I asked Emily what was going on. Even Plácido Domingo didn't have that many fans waiting at the stage door when he arrived. Emily explained that when the recording had aired, people had heard

Pollyanne braying and had rung the BBC or the Royal Opera House to find out what was going on. So many people had called that they ended up jamming the switchboards. When they found out that a live donkey was in the opera, they asked when Pollyanne would next be performing so they could meet her. Ticket sales had soared, partly due to Pollyanne. And unbeknownst to me, a journalist from the *Telegraph* had reviewed the performance and mentioned Pollyanne, so even more people found out. Emily told me the Royal Opera House bosses were probably pleased about the extra exposure it gave the production.

Even Plácido Domingo had been interviewed about the incident – Emily said he had told a journalist that Pollyanne was the only creature that had ever outsung him. What praise! I couldn't believe it. Maybe Pollyanne's braying had been a good thing after all. The whole cast and crew seemed to be buzzing, and many admitted that they'd been on the Island Farm website and adopted Pollyanne to celebrate the show's success.

Once it was show time I quickly forgot about it all and sat in my seat by Pollyanne's pen to wait for her to finish her scene. I held my breath when it got to the duet, but this time Pollyanne didn't make a sound. Jane joked that Pollyanne's friends in the audience would be disappointed, but I was just pleased everything had gone smoothly.

After the final curtain I hung around for a while, chatting with Emily. When we finally left, most people had already gone home and I thought with relief that it would be much easier to get Pollyanne back into the lorry than it had been to get her out. But when I opened the stage door, I found that there was still a crowd of people outside. I thought they must have been waiting for Plácido Domingo so I told them that he'd already gone back to his hotel – I didn't see the point in them waiting around in the cold for no reason. They just laughed. 'It's Pollyanne we've been waiting for!' I had been shocked to see so many people waiting for us in the afternoon, but to see even more waiting late at night blew me away.

They all had their *Pagliacci* programmes with them and a girl stepped forward to ask if she could have Pollyanne's autograph. I didn't know what to say! I'd never heard of a donkey being asked for a signature before but I didn't want to disappoint the girl so I asked her to just give me a minute. I walked over to the lorry with Pollyanne and opened the passenger side. In the footwell was a bottle of hoof oil and I carefully opened the top and poured some on a cloth I had in my jacket pocket. I rubbed the oil on the underside of Pollyanne's foot and then told the girl to put her programme down on the pavement. I lifted Pollyanne's front foot and placed it down on the programme, like a stamp. When I lifted her foot, the girl was left with a perfect impression of Pollyanne's hoof-print. 'Just be careful until it dries,' I told her. Before I knew it everyone was waving their programmes in the air and shouting, 'Me next!'

'What have I started?' I thought to myself, then instructed everyone to line up on the pavement with their programmes on the ground in front of them. Then

I got on my hands and knees, and taking Pollyanne's oiled foot, pressed it down on each programme in turn. By the time I'd finished I was worn out but at least Pollyanne's fans were happy. I gave Pollyanne a stroke and then led her up her ramp onto the lorry, while her fans photographed the whole thing. I didn't know what to say to them really – they would have liked to spend hours with her but we had to get back. I said a quick goodbye and watched them wave as we pulled away.

I was looking forward to telling Stuart about what had happened, and what Plácido Domingo had said about Pollyanne to that journalist. Plácido was such a nice guy – I'd gained so much respect for him through the rehearsals and performances. He said hello to me without fail when we passed backstage and he'd give Pollyanne the odd stroke too.

Our final performance was a very emotional night. We had all bonded so much that it was hard saying goodbye. Pollyanne and I had got into a routine and were going to miss our twice-weekly trips to London. I was particularly going to miss Jane and Emily, but they both said they would keep in touch and would plan a trip to the sanctuary soon.

I think Linda and Gaggy were secretly happy that our time at the Royal Opera House was coming to an end because they had been doing all my work on performance days. I didn't know if Pollyanne would ever get another chance to perform on such a huge stage and it made me a little bit sad to think that she might never get to step out into the limelight again.

8

Silent Night

'Stuart, *hurry up*! We need to leave now otherwise we'll
be late.'

Usually I was the late one, but for once it was Stuart
holding us up. He was still in the office, busily stuffing
envelopes with donkey adoption packs. We had been
inundated with orders from people who had left their
Christmas shopping to the last minute – and we had
just twenty-four hours left to process them all and get
them in the post in time for Christmas delivery. Every

year it is the same mad panic to get them all out in time.

Snow had been falling for about an hour now. It started just I was getting the donkeys in from the paddocks and was now settling, frosting the trees and buildings with a thin layer of white. The donkeys were enchanted by the spectacle – staring in wonder at the flakes as they landed gently on their noses, licking them off as they trotted home to their stables for the night.

I heard the office door open and then shut, so I knew Stuart would be with me once he'd locked up. Pollyanne was already in the lorry, along with our two sheep, waiting for us both to take them to their first Christmas engagement of the year: a nativity play for the children at Madgalen Road Evangelical Free Church.

Reindeer are in prime demand at Christmas, of course, but donkeys come a close second and several of ours had been out on jobs that week. Charlie and Jack had been into primary schools, Queen had been guest of honour at a Christmas fête and Bruno had been to two Brownie meetings. I'd chosen Pollyanne for the biggest job, though, because I knew she would do it well and the children would love her.

The church was only eleven miles up the road, which I was glad of because the snow was falling quite heavily as we made our way there. As soon as we parked up outside the church and unloaded Pollyanne, the church's pastor came out and beckoned us to bring Pollyanne and the sheep inside, out of the snow. Pollyanne's role, of course, was to carry Mary to Bethlehem and during the service she would lead the congregation out of the church to a purpose-built stable in the churchyard, where the nativity would be re-enacted.

The pastor introduced us to the volunteers who would be playing Mary, Joseph and the innkeeper. I was relieved to see that the actress playing Mary was a slight woman with a fluffy pillow for the bump of baby Jesus – Pollyanne's a sturdy little thing but I would have worried about her carrying a real pregnant woman. I was keen to keep the animals inside, out of the cold, for as long as possible so I nipped out myself to have a look at the stable before the celebrations began. I was amazed at what they'd achieved. The stable looked so authentic, with straw on the ground and a manger set up in the middle of the structure. It all looked so solid and cosy it made me reflect, not for the first time, that our own stables at the sanctuary desperately needed rebuilding. There was already a little calf in there to keep Pollyanne and the sheep company – all the scene needed was a baby Jesus. 'Mary' explained that there would be a doll hidden behind the calf's feeding trough and that she would whip it out at the appropriate moment during the performance.

When it was time for the service to begin, I helped Mary up onto Pollyanne's back and told Joseph how to lead her. I would follow discreetly, just in case I was needed. I was surprised by how many people were crammed inside the church – it was full to capacity and people were spilling out onto the street. Luckily everyone was in such good spirits that they didn't seem to mind the cold. I could hear the chatter of all the excited children in the congregation – they had seen Pollyanne standing up near the altar and were eager to know what was going to happen. The pastor welcomed everybody and said some lovely words about the meaning of Christmas. The children were silenced as he began to tell the familiar story, and – when the moment came – they all followed dutifully as Pollyanne, Mary and Joseph walked down the aisle and out to the stable. In the time I'd been inside the church, the snow had really started to come down and the scene in front of us was picture-perfect. A pristine layer of snow covered the stable and hundreds of tiny fairy lights twinkled in the surrounding trees. Pollyanne stood proudly behind Mary and Joseph, looking out at the assembled crowd. No one spoke – they just stayed for a while then moved round so that the next people in the queue could see. We must have stood there for well over an hour and Pollyanne stayed perfectly still the entire time. Nothing would put her off, not even the frisky little calf, who kept trying to lick her. Whenever he moved too close, she just nudged him with her nose and gave a quiet *hee-haw*. He would quickly step back and then, five minutes later, try again . . . with the same result: nudge; *hee-haw*. If there was a thought bubble above Polly-anne's head, I'm sure it would have said: *Amateurs! Tsk.* Luckily the sheep were content to munch on the straw and barely registered the crowd of people watching them eat.

By the time the last family had disappeared back into the church it was getting late. When the pastor came over to thank us for taking part, he said that over 250 people had come to the service – quite a remarkable turnout.

The next morning I woke to an eerie light in my bed-room. I jumped out of bed like a small child on Christmas Day and ran to the window: the snow had continued to fall and the whole sanctuary was com-pletely blanketed in what looked like at least a foot of it.

I stood there for a moment and took it all in ... it was breathtaking; so bright it almost hurt my eyes.

Beautiful it may have been, but I knew the day was going to be a challenge. There was no way the donkeys could go into the fields – their coats are not waterproof and they would catch a chill. And I knew from experience we'd have to stay on our guard against their water troughs freezing up. I made my way to the office to put the kettle on – there was no way I was facing this weather without a hot cup of tea to warm me up. I was just undoing the door when I noticed a sack hanging on the main gate, covered in snow. Maybe we'd had a delivery and the driver had been in a rush? I walked over and grabbed it, but before I could untie the sack something moved inside, kicking against my leg. Whatever was in this sack was alive and it wanted to get out.

I laid the sack gently on the snow and, ever so slowly, opened the top a fraction. Nothing immediately jumped out, so I opened it slightly more and leant forward to peer inside. Looking back at me, blinking and shivering, were two gorgeous baby rabbits. One was white with grey patches with its ears pricked straight upright and the other was a dark brown colour with floppy ears. They must have been absolutely freezing! I carried the sack back to the office. It looked like Island Farm had two new residents.

Five minutes later, Gaggy arrived at the office. I had a mug of steaming hot tea ready for him and I had already named the rabbits: Holly and Ivy. Perfect, considering they'd arrived just days before Christmas. I told him about my discovery and we realised that they must have been in that sack, in the freezing cold, for at least eight hours. Sadly, finding abandoned animals tied to the gate wasn't an unusual occurrence, but to do it in such bad weather conditions was particularly heartless. I was surprised the baby rabbits had survived – they could easily have frozen to death or been eaten by a fox.

I will never understand why people choose not to come and talk to us directly if they have animals they want us to take in. I suppose it's guilt and shame that drive them to be so covert about it, but there is no need. We always take in animals, no questions asked. I bet if people had the courage to do it face-to-face, they would leave us with a clearer conscience.

Thankfully the tiny rabbits didn't seem any the worse for wear and we made them comfortable in one of our spare rabbit hutches and then headed over to the barn to prepare for a carol service that was to take place later in the day. We had never held a service at the sanctuary before, but I felt that it was something we should do this year. We had so much to be thankful for. I may not get to church every Sunday, but God always provides for us and I wanted to give something back to the people who I knew remembered our work in their prayers.

The vicar, Reverend Janice Chilton – Linda's mum – would be leading the short service. She is a close friend of the sanctuary and loves the donkeys. Afterwards there would be mince pies and drinks. Our first task was to decorate the barn so that it looked Christmassy. Our supporters had donated their unwanted decorations and one chap had given us a magnificent seven-foot tree – which immediately made the barn look more festive. Then we hung string after string of fairy lights around the barn's walls and ceilings so that it would look sparkly and magical once it was dark. We were just about finished when Linda popped by with Pollyanne hot on her heels. Pollyanne is a very nosy donkey and doesn't like to miss out on anything – she must have figured out that something unusual was going on and followed Linda to try and get in on the action. She had a good sniff of the Christmas tree and seemed very taken with the gold baubles, nudging them with her nose and apparently entranced by her reflection in their surface. I left her to it for a moment and turned to finish attaching some holly to one of the beams … when I looked again, she was standing there innocently with a string of bright red tinsel between her teeth. She must have pulled it from one of the branches – we were lucky the whole tree hadn't collapsed on top of her!

'Pollyanne! What are you playing at?' I asked her,

shaking my head. I took the tinsel from her and couldn't resist tying it around her neck. She trotted over to show off her new bling to Linda. Such an attention seeker!

The service went off without a hitch. After all those trips out over the preceding few weeks, visiting nativities and carol concerts all over the place, it was lovely to celebrate all together at the sanctuary with our friends and supporters. And all the donkeys, of course! We couldn't squeeze them all into the barn for the service, but our visitors went to visit them in the stables when it was over and they certainly got a lot of Christmas love and attention.

Before long it was Christmas Day – the only day of the year when we are officially closed to the public. Having said that, we do allow people who have adopted one of our donkeys to come along for a special Christmas Day visit. Arthur and May were here again, they come every Christmas Day, as do Richard and Marlene and Peggy and Rachel. We do try give the donkeys a Christmas Day to remember and, as was tradition, I wore a rather fetching Santa hat.

'Merry Christmas, Pollyanne!' one little boy called out and asked if I could pick him up so he could stroke her nose. His mum handed him a carrot and together we fed her. Others had brought presents for the donkeys, too: gingernut biscuits and apples wrapped up in colourful paper. We made sure that everyone had something and no one was left out, but there's always one or two who try to sneak more than their fair share. One visitor had brought along a Christmas cake which she passed round – I took a slice eagerly, as I hadn't eaten lunch yet. I only managed a mouthful before Queen swooped in and wolfed it up, right from my hand. So cheeky! I couldn't be cross though – it was Christmas Day, after all.

'Go on, then,' I said with a smile, giving her a quick stroke on her nose. Before long all the donkeys crowded round me and I was stroking and tickling them all: 'Merry Christmas, Queen! Merry Christmas, Tracy! Merry Christmas, Pollyanne!'

9

Foreign Shores

'C'mon, Diana,' I sighed. 'Let's get this all tidied up.'

It had rained torrentially during the night and the girls' stable had sprung another leak in the roof. Poor old Diana had spent the night standing in soggy straw and was looking quite sorry for herself this morning. I didn't blame her. I hated that we weren't always able to protect the donkeys from the worst of the elements. I'd try and patch up the hole, of course, but these days the roof was pretty much all patch and I knew it wouldn't hold out for much longer. But we didn't have anything like the funds available to pay for a new roof. Let alone a completely new stable, which is what we really needed. I led Diana out into the paddock and set to work clearing out all of the wet straw before I got out the ladder and headed up to the roof to check out the damage. As I surveyed the roof, noticing with relief that the last patch I'd done seemed to be holding up, I made a mental list of all the work that needed doing at the sanctuary. New boys' and girls' stables; replacing some of the fencing around the paddock; mending the door on the barn ... all basic stuff we needed to sort out asap in order to make sure the donkeys were safe and happy. And then there was the wishlist: a new visitors' centre of some sort; a better office for Stuart and Wendy ... My mind reeled. How would ever find the money to do all this? It just didn't seem possible. We had enough funds to last another two months but that was it. Sponsorship numbers were down, we had more donkeys than we ever had before – I never turn away a needy animal –

and that meant food and vet bills were higher than they'd ever been.

As I came down the ladder to fetch my tools, Stuart called me over to the office. Kay had been on the phone – could I call her back? I certainly could – at least if Pollyanne had another job we'd maybe be able to get the fencing sorted.

I imagined Kay would tell me that Pollyanne was wanted for a small part on TV or something – something with a small fee that would help us out for a week or so – but what she actually had to say almost completely knocked me off my feet. It could be the answer to all our problems!

I went outside and found Stuart, Gaggy, Wendy and Linda taking a break over by the barn. We'd all been working extra-long hours recently and it was starting to catch up with us. None of us has holidays as such, and days off are a rarity anyway. I told them that Kay had just called to say that we'd been offered a big job. It was for Pollyanne to perform in another opera – but this time

she'd be travelling to Norway to perform in a new theatre that had been built there. When I said the word
'Norway', all four of them opened their mouths in
shock. I smiled, knowing I must have looked just the
same when Kay told me the news five minutes earlier.
And I had one more shock for them: I held up a piece of
paper and told them that they were going to pay us the
amount of money that was written there.

'How much?!' was Gaggy's reply.

'That's unbelievable . . . *unbelievable*,' said Linda, shaking her head.

'Let's not get carried away with it,' I said, trying to
keep their feet on the ground. I told them I'd need to be
away with Pollyanne for a full month, so the four of
them would have to run things here in my absence. It
was a fantastic opportunity but it would be hard on
everyone. I'd never even been abroad before! Pollyanne
might have a passport, but I didn't. I'd have to get one
sorted as soon as possible.

All four of them thought it was too good an

opportunity to miss, in spite of the challenges it would present. I was glad they were up for it because I was feeling excited about it already. Pollyanne would be an international star! She had never been on a live cargo plane before but I was sure she'd be fine and it sounded far more appealing than the alternative – driving her in the lorry through France, Belgium, Holland, Germany and Denmark before getting a boat over to Norway.

I rang Kay back and told her the good news. She was so excited and said she'd send over a mountain of paper-work straight away. Transporting a donkey abroad is not the easiest thing to do. She would also book our flights, as she would be coming with us for the first couple of days to make sure that we settled in okay.

In the weeks to come I made a start on all the jobs around the sanctuary that I had been putting off. I didn't want to go to Norway for a month and leave Gaggy and Linda to do it all. I painted the fences, mended the roof of the chicken coop and signed the invoices that needed paying. I even surprised Wendy by spending a whole afternoon in the office sorting out paperwork. One night we all decided to go the Red Lion for a meal to reward ourselves for the hard work we had been putting in. As I sat at the table, I realised how much I was going to miss everyone. They all promised to ring me loads and keep me informed and I made them swear that if one of the old donkeys got sick they'd let me know straight away. I couldn't bear the thought of coming back and finding out one of them had passed away.

A few days later, I went down to the post office in the village to pick up a form for my passport. Imagine if we went to all the trouble of getting Pollyanne ready to travel and forgot about me! When I got back to the office, I cleared some space on a desk in the office and set about filling in all the details. Just as I was getting into my stride, the phone rang. It was Kay.

'John, I'm afraid I've got some bad news,' she said. 'There's no point in me beating about the bush: the trip's been cancelled.'

My stomach lurched. I could barely take it in as she told me that the Agricultural Ministry in Norway wouldn't allow us to enter the country. They were concerned about a recent outbreak of blue-tongue disease in the UK – donkeys can be carriers even though they can't get it themselves. I could kind of see their logic, but I was devastated.

It felt as if we'd been robbed. We had come so close to earning enough money to solve all our financial worries for the foreseeable future. I didn't know what I was going to say to the others – they'd be heartbroken too. I wandered over to the far paddock and spent some time with Matthew and Mickey, a bonded pair of mistreated donkeys who had arrived a few weeks earlier. Matthew had bad scarring running up his back and Mickey was extremely thin due to problems with his guts. They were sharing their paddock with two Shetland ponies – the only ponies we'd had since Island Farm Donkey Sanctuary was first established. Bob and Betty were lovely little things but didn't like people making sudden movements around them, a clear sign that they'd been hit in the past. If I wanted to get near them I had to crouch down and move extremely slowly so as to not scare them off. Luckily they had been getting on well with Matthew and Mickey.

I found a carrot and snapped it into four roughly equally pieces. Their ears pricked up at the sound and they turned as one in my direction.

'Matthew, Mickey, Bob, Betty ... come here.'

I held one piece out on the palm of my left hand. Mickey took one step forward, looked at Matthew, then another step, looked at Matthew, and so on until he was an arm's length away – at which point Matthew clearly decided he didn't want to be left out. He trotted up, walked straight past Mickey, and took the carrot from my hand with a practised sweep of his tongue. Mickey looked a bit miffed to say the least but I took another piece and held it out to him. He was still a bit nervous but he gobbled it up quick-smart anyway. Bob and Betty were watching with interest but I could tell they didn't yet feel confident enough to approach me. I bent down and rolled a piece each towards their feet, and they ate them up in seconds. It was a simple act of affection, the sort of thing I do each day at the sanctuary, but somehow it helped me put the disappointment of Norway in perspective. We would just have to find another way to make a future for ourselves.

In the next few weeks the weather grew worse. It was only mid-October but the temperature was already dropping rapidly and I found that I struggled to stay warm as I went about my work in the stables day after day. I was busy trying to repair them, at least partly, before the winter really took hold. A couple of the stables were so unsafe that I'd had to rearrange the sleeping arrangements for the boys. I hated the way things were but there was no prospect of us being able to afford the new building work we so desperately needed, especially since the Norway trip was cancelled. I just had to keep patching things up, staving off the inevitable.

We needed a miracle, that was for sure.

I opened the door to the office one afternoon expecting to find Stuart at work, but he was nowhere to be seen. Spread out on his desk were dozens of printouts of the best donkey shelters money can buy. Stuart must have spent the morning on the Internet, researching. He might as well have been looking at millionaire's mansions. I picked them up, one after another. Top of the range stables – they were amazing. Just looking at them made me feel guilty that our donkeys lived in such old ramshackle affairs ... I felt a surge of anger and was about to hurl them all in the bin, when Stuart stepped through the door with a huge grin on his face. I asked him what he was playing at – had he lost his mind? – but he just laughed, handed me a letter and told me to read it.

The letter was addressed to me. It said that two benefactors were going to give us some money. Good news, I thought. Then I saw the amount they were donating. *Fifty thousand pounds*! I couldn't believe it.

'Are you sure this is right?' I asked Stuart. Maybe they'd added a few too many zeros. Maybe the whole thing was a hoax. They were surely trying to put me in an early grave.

Stuart nodded. He had rung them up and spoken to them at length. It was a genuine offer. The letter was from a very generous trust who had received the money from a lady who had passed away. It was so unexpected, I was speechless.

I took the printouts I was holding and threw them in the bin, much to Stuart's dismay. They were fancy enough, but we needed stables that would last year after year. Straight away ideas started forming in my head, so I picked up a pencil from the desk and started sketching away. We were going to have the best donkey shelters money could buy! No longer would the donkeys be kept in pairs or fours at night, we would have one giant stables for the girls, another for the boys. They would offer enough space for the donkeys to move around indoors when the weather was bad and they would be easy to maintain. There was absolutely no way were going to have wooden shelters either – only steel ones would do.

My sketches were very rough but Stuart could see the sort of thing I had in mind. He said he would do some research into planning permission and find an architect and a builder to quote for the work. If I could have had it my way I would have jumped in the tractor and bull-dozed the old stables within the hour, but realistically it was probably going to take at least six months to sort everything out. I was going to do my best to keep every-thing moving along, though. I couldn't wait to see Pollyanne and her friends in their new home. I was so happy! I went back out to finish up my jobs. Now I knew the stables only needed to last a little while longer, fixing them became less depressing.

10

Moving House

In a matter of weeks a local architect had taken my drawings and turned them into something beautiful. We could comfortably house fifty donkeys in each.

The plans were approved much more quickly than we anticipated, so it wasn't long before we could begin construction work. To prepare the ground for the building work, the vast majority of the existing stables had been demolished and the few that remained were now full to bursting. The donkeys would be very glad to be out of their crowded temporary stables.

The day the steel framework was due to arrive I woke up extra early as they were expected before eight and I had to make sure all the donkeys were fed and in their paddocks before everything kicked off. The three-man construction team arrived on time, so I quickly stuck the kettle on and rustled up some bacon sarnies for sustenance. I had a feeling they'd need it, and sure enough, just as they took their first bites, a wagon appeared round the corner loaded up with steel. We all helped unload them – and, boy, were they heavy!

After that I left them to it and got on with the million and one other things I still had to do around the sanctuary. I was very excited because we had a Championship Donkey Show coming up on the Saturday and I had decided to enter two-year-old Barron, who had arrived at the sanctuary twelve months ago. We had taken him to a few small shows in the last few months but the Championship Donkey Show was as big as it gets. I needed to spend some time with him today to make sure he was ready and to remind him what he had to do in the ring. Stuart would pretend to be a judge, checking him from head to toe.

Barron was one of the donkeys we had rescued from the travellers' horse fair up in Stow-on-the-Wold. It is a huge event and it takes place twice a year. Hundreds of horses and donkeys are paraded up and down the street – ridden bare-backed or with a racing cart attached to them – before being offered for sale. Poor Barron was very young and yet he was being ridden by a heavy man whose weight he couldn't bear. I found it heartbreaking to watch but people around me were cheering him on. I bought him then and there. I didn't ever want him to have to experience being ridden that way again. Thankfully he was still in decent health but he was a very nervous thing and if you so much as raised your voice to him he would start to shiver. It took us a long time to gain his confidence, but once we did he turned out to be a real winner. Barron is one of the best show donkeys we've ever had at the sanctuary – everything is in perfect proportion and the way he moves is just right. He is the kind of donkey a top breeder would give their right arm to own and you can tell just from looking at him that he was from good breeding. He has won a few rosettes in smaller shows, but I wasn't sure how he would fare in the Championship Donkey Show competing against the best donkeys in the UK.

As the days went by the shelters started to take shape and by the end of the week the outside frames had been constructed, with only the panelling and roofs left to do. We tried to give the lads a wide berth so they could get on with what they were doing, but we made sure to take them tea and coffee every few hours and some of our volunteers even dropped by with homemade cakes and biscuits for them to show their appreciation.

The donkeys were very intrigued by the work, and would trot as slowly as possible to their paddocks in the morning so that they could have a look and take it all in. The cheekier donkeys tried to dip under the rope to get a closer look so I had to keep my eye on them.

On the day of the Championship, Linda and I got dressed up in our finest togs to make sure we didn't let Barron down. Linda had spent hours getting him ready the day before, so this morning his coat was glossy, his tail combed and his hooves blacked to a brilliant shine: in short, he looked immaculate. I ironed my best shirt, made sure my suit was pressed and dusted off my bowler hat.

I love these shows and it's great to be with fellow donkey owners, some of whom have become good friends over the years. The event itself is much like a dog show – each class is called into a ring and the judges go from donkey to donkey, checking them over from their teeth to their feet. The donkeys have to stay completely still while this is happening and then do a lap of the ring so the judges can see how they move. There can be quite a lot of donkeys in each class so it's always a great feeling if your donkey is picked out for a rosette.

That day I was hoping that Barron would pick up a rosette of some description – but he was up against some amazing donkeys, from the best breeders in the country. The other donkeys had never witnessed cruelty like Barron had; they'd spent their lives being looked after well – they had never been beaten and humiliated. So when the judge stepped forward to crown Barron British Supreme Champion Donkey, I felt proud as punch of all he had achieved. Given the terrible start he had in life, it was nothing short of remarkable. Barron's certificate and champion rosette would sit pride of place alongside Pollyanne's framed paper cuttings in the office from now on.

The stables were completed in twelve days flat and finished at 3 p.m. on a Friday afternoon. We all congregated in the yard to watch the final piece of roofing being slotted into place, arms linked in a sign of unity. As soon as the crew disappeared round the corner in their van for the last time, we all hurried over to inspect the new shelters properly.

We broke apart and walked over to the girls' stable

first. It was absolutely huge. We walked around in silence, running our hands over the steelwork, admiring it all. We couldn't wait to show the donkeys. After five or ten minutes we grabbed some wheelbarrows from the barn, filled them with straw and set about preparing the floor. We worked in silence, concentrating hard to get the shelter ready for occupation. Once we'd finished the girls' new home, we repeated the task over in the boys'. After goodness knows how many hours of intensive work, the shelters were ready: we went to the front paddock to get the girls.

Lady, Loppy and Queen were leading the herd today, with Pollyanne and Tracy not far behind them. The rest followed in a line, as we would expect. Some of the newer donkeys were slower on the uptake as they'd been grazing at the far side so had to move fast to catch up with the others. We had created a walkway using rope, to guide them all in the right direction, but some still wandered astray, clearly searching for their old stables.

When the first few donkeys reached the new shelters they were cautious at first, sniffing them as if to check that they were okay, before heading towards the nearest feeding bowls. Pollyanne, Tracy and the others followed suit, until all forty-two of them were happily munching under the roof. There was still plenty of room; we could easily fit another twenty donkeys in if we'd needed to. We had fixed a metal fence around the perimeter of the shelter which gave the girls some yard space too – they could choose whether to be underneath the roof or out-doors. As I turned to go, Midge came and put her head over the top of the fence, wanting a stroke. I couldn't resist, she is such a little sweetheart. We had rescued her in conjunction with the RSPCA from a barren scrap of land. Her owners had smashed all her teeth out with a metal bar. Our vets couldn't believe the physical state she was in, let alone the terrible psychological damage she had sustained. We paid a great deal of money to repair her mouth as best as possible. She used to flinch every time anyone came close, and to approach her I would have to get on my hands and knees so I wasn't a threat. It took a long time but she learnt to trust me and eventually felt confident enough to approach me herself. Since that day we'd never looked back.

The new shelters were a real boost for everyone associated with the sanctuary but we soon discovered another reason to celebrate: we were going to get our very own visitors' centre. A local primary school was thinking of selling or scrapping an old mobile classroom, but someone had come up with the bright idea that we might be able to put it to good use. I just couldn't believe it when they rang. All we had to do was pay for the transportation cost; what we got in return was worth ten times that. Once we'd cleaned it up inside, and added a fresh lick of paint, it was as good as new. It had two working toilets, a main room and a little stock room that we could easily turn into a small kitchen if we wanted to. It was going to be a godsend whenever the weather took a turn for the worse because visitors would no longer have to make a dash for their cars – they could take a seat inside and watch the donkeys from the window until it stopped raining.

Once the visitors' centre was completely finished we decided to hold a special opening day. Pollyanne would be the main attraction as the local children always loved seeing her. She couldn't cut the ribbon, though, so we invited our local MP Ed Vaizey to do the honours for her. Ed is a huge supporter of the sanctuary and always helps us when he can and with his help the ceremony was a great success. We were so busy we almost ran out of refreshments, and our supporters had outdone themselves with cakes and all kinds of baked goods. Adoption forms were in high demand and we were rushed off our feet all day. We felt truly blessed.

11

Whodunnit?

I was in the office riffling through my paperwork. I piled up any invoices or receipts to one side and ripped out any articles featuring Pollyanne from the many news-papers I had somehow accumulated. I propped up the programme from Barron's championship show to show Gaggy later.

Wendy's phone rang. I carried on, trying to ignore it, but whoever was at the other end wasn't giving up. Eventually it clicked over to the answering machine.

Whodunnit?

'John? It's Cyril, mate. Please call me.'

I rushed to pick up the receiver – Cyril and I go way back. He runs the Warren Hill Goat Sanctuary, about five miles away from Island Farm, and we help each other out when we can. We hadn't chatted for a while – both of us had been so busy with our sanctuaries in the last few months and we were overdue a catch-up.

That morning, Cyril explained, he had gone to check on his goats and found the padlock was missing from the door leading to their pen. He opened the door and took a quick head count. Two of them were gone. A pool of blood lay in the corner. It couldn't have been a fox because it was two of the adult goats who were missing, and it would take a hell of a fox to bring one of them down. Cyril thought intruders must have broken in during the night, slit the throats of his goats and taken the bodies away with them. The police were there now, checking for fingerprints. He was devastated, and I just couldn't think of the right words to say.

It had shaken Cyril to the core to think that animals

he had rescued had been murdered like that and I felt sick thinking about it. The people who had done this were capable of anything. They obviously had no conscience.

I offered to help in any way I could, but really there was nothing I could do other than lend a sympathetic ear. I couldn't imagine how he felt. He wanted to warn me so I could be on my guard, and he would call again in a few days' time if he had any news. I just hoped the police would catch whoever was responsible.

I was glad that I lived on site, to protect the donkeys if need be. I don't know why anyone would target us – we don't have anything worth stealing. Stuart's PC is ancient and we don't even have lots of scrap metal knocking around. Nevertheless, we have had intruders in the past but thanks to our terrific guard dogs, Corky, Patch, Tubby and Candy, they never managed to get near the donkeys. The dogs stand guard at the gate after everything has been locked up for the night and if anyone tries so much as to get in, they bark their heads off. By night Corky, Patch, Tubby and Candy could be mistaken for menacing Alsatians or Dobermans but in truth they are tiny terriers. We don't allow them to wander round the sanctuary during visiting hours but they keep me company before we open up. They never get in the way of the donkeys. They are softies really; they love a cuddle or a scratch between their ears. Their favourite game is tag, which they play with each other, running around the yard like crazy. Patch usually starts it off, then Tubby chases him, followed by Corky and Candy. When a game is full swing, I try not to make any moves for fear that a dog will come tearing out of nowhere and smack you in the legs. Not at all desirable if you're carrying a mug of hot tea!

I found Gaggy outside and told him what had happened at Warren Hill. He asked whether we should postpone the photoshoot we had arranged to take some new pictures of Charlie and Jack for their adoption packs. I thought it best to get on with it: we couldn't do anything for Cyril, and Charlie and Jack were ready to go. They had been brushed and were looking smart but natural in the paddock – we didn't want to overdo it. Getting them to look at the camera was tricky – they were mostly interested in the grass. I ended up on my back by Jack's two front feet, holding the rope steady. Gaggy called out Jack's name. He looked up for a split second, and we got the perfect shot. We went through the same procedure with Charlie, who was far more difficult, but eventually Gaggy got the shot and declared that it was a wrap.

We were pleased with the photos but the day did end with some more bad news from Cyril. The police had stopped a car acting suspiciously that night but had let it go. When they were told about the break-in, they managed to track it down again and found the goats' bodies inside. Poor Cyril had to identify the bodies. There wasn't, however, going to be any prosecution. It was truly awful.

Working 8 a.m. till 8 p.m. every day means that I don't have much time for relaxing in front of the television, but

Whodunnit?

I have enjoyed the odd episode of *Midsomer Murders* over the years so I was particularly pleased when Pollyanne and a few of her friends were asked to appear in an episode.

It turned out that the location team from the production company had been on a secret trip to the sanctuary to look around and meet the donkeys. They hadn't let on as to who they were. They had taken lots of photos and quizzed us about Pollyanne's work at the Royal Opera House – I didn't remember them, but we get loads of visitors taking pictures and asking questions so it wouldn't have seemed out of the ordinary. Apparently they had loved Island Farm, especially the stables, and they wanted to film part of the episode here. I was so excited when I heard that I clean forgot that the old stables they thought were so perfect for the shoot no longer existed. It wasn't until I glanced up and saw Pollyanne and Tracy under the new shelters that it dawned on me. I explained to the company that we had replaced the old stables with two modern shelters. They were disappointed because the the storyline called for a more run-down and old-fashioned setting. I thought the whole thing might be called off, but to my relief they still wanted to use our donkeys. They just needed to solve the location problem and a few days later they called to say that they had found some stables in Bledlow Ridge that would perfect.

Pollyanne and eleven of her friends would be appearing in an episode called 'Echoes of the Dead' – we would be needed for three full days. Linda and I thought long and hard about which donkeys would we take – they needed to be confident, happy to travel and reliable. We both agreed on the first six: Pollyanne, Tracy, Queen, Diane, Charlie and Jack. After than it got tricky. I really wanted to take Loppy, but Linda thought she might be too big. Linda wanted to take Betty and Midge, but I thought they wouldn't like being away from the sanctuary – and she thought the same of my next two suggestions Polo and Perry. In the end we ended up choosing Brandy, Misty, Chocolate, Mr

Crusty, Bunty and Gerald. Six girls and six boys – perfect.

So our opera star was making the move into television – how exciting! Some of her friends had done a bit of telly work before but this was going to be a first for Pollyanne. I couldn't wait to tell the visitors and sanctuary supporters so that everyone would watch.

The day before the filming was very frantic for me, Linda and Gaggy – we spent nearly all afternoon grooming all twelve donkeys to make sure they looked perfect. I think they all sensed that something special was going to happen. The next morning it took hardly any time to load the donkeys into the lorry and set off on the twenty-mile drive to Bledlow Ridge.

There must have been at least fifty people milling about the location, which did look a lot like Island Farm before its makeover. There were static caravans dotted about which I guessed were for the actors and I could see signs for wardrobe and makeup as well as huge vans which were filled with recording equipment. Everyone seemed to be in a rush, and to begin with we weren't sure where to go. Thankfully, a young girl called Hannah came over to explain that she would be looking after us and making sure that we went to the right place at the right time. Filming for TV means a lot of waiting around, she said, but there were secure paddocks the donkeys could graze in when they weren't doing their scenes and there was a van selling hot drinks and food if we got peckish.

Hannah took us over to the paddock as we had at least an hour before we were needed on set and I released the donkeys, but made sure they kept their collars on so it would be easy to get them later. She asked which donkey I had picked for the principal role which was a surprise because I hadn't known I had to pick one! But it was a pretty easy decision to make – Pollyanne.

Filming for a TV programme is very quick and there's little time to practise. With our opera performances we had lots of rehearsals before the opening night but for *Midsomer Murders* the director wanted us to get it right first time. I wasn't given a full script as the scenes at the donkey sanctuary would only make up a small part of the whole story and the other locations were being filmed on other days.

The confusing thing was that the scenes weren't going to be shot in sequence, so in one scene they would be talking about the a character being murdered, and then after that we filmed a scene where that same character was still alive! We weren't told who the murderer was so I kept looking at the cast and trying to figure it out, even though I was missing most of the plot.

In the episode, the murder victim's best friend worked at a donkey sanctuary, so Pollyanne and her gang were integral to the plot and I was pleased when the director asked me for advice on how the donkeys should be handled by the actress playing the vet so that it looked authentic. After listening to what I had to say, she was allowed to deviate from her script, which I must admit gave me a bit of a buzz, as it made me a kind of unofficial scriptwriter.

In the scene with the vet, the donkey's owner is played by Pam Ferris – the actress who played Ma in *The Darling Buds of May*. I was a bit starstruck at first because I used to love that show when it was on. Misty played the injured donkey, although they renamed her Rosie.

Linda and I had to be very quick and do whatever the director said while filming these scenes – we spent so much time standing in bushes, lying on the ground. Even though you can't see us, we were there holding on to the donkeys, making sure they stayed put and didn't wander off. For the vet scene I was crouched in a giant shrub holding on to Misty's lead rope – I didn't half get cramp in my legs while I was waiting for them to finish!

Once the director called 'cut', I came out of the shrub and they asked me whether what the women had said sounded right, I said it did and that was that, on to the next scene.

We filmed the opening sequence next, with all the donkeys grazing in a huge paddock with the sanctuary buildings behind them. It was important that none of us were on camera so we had to leave them to it and move as far back as possible, out of view. Easy enough! If there's one thing donkeys know how to do without direction, it's graze! The next shot was of one of the main characters cycling through the sanctuary so I had to leave Pollyanne and Tracy outside a stable, munching on some straw. You only see the back view of them at this stage. As one of the characters cycles down the lane you see more donkeys in the adjoining paddock, but we just used the same donkeys again and again – we had to make our twelve donkeys play several parts.

We managed to fit a lot into the first day so we were absolutely shattered when it came to driving home. By the time we arrived back at the sanctuary and had unloaded the donkeys, fed and watered them, I was dead on my feet. I collapsed on my bed without even bothering to get changed.

The next morning I felt much better and had a quick catch-up with Gaggy before we set off. He had nothing major to report from the day but was pleased to hear our first day had gone well.

When we arrived at the location, we got the donkeys out in double-quick time and led them over to Hannah who was waiting for us by the barn. This time Pollyanne was in a crucial scene with one of the main suspects, who was being questioned by DCI Barnaby. Pollyanne (or Walter, as she was named in the script!) was as good as gold, but in the background Charlie and Jack were poking their heads over the stable door, hee-hawing and trying to push each other out the way. I thought the director would want to reshoot the scene but thankfully he said he liked seeing the donkeys' mischievous side.

Afterwards Neil Dudgeon, the actor who plays DCI Barnaby, came over to chat to me about the donkeys. He seemed a really nice, genuine bloke. He was relatively new to it all because he'd only just started filming his first episodes playing the lead after John Nettles had retired. He was so convincing when questioning the actor in Pollyanne's scene that he'd become my number 1 suspect. I kept trying to think of the practicalities: who would be physically strong enough to strangle the victim ... I had to keep reminding myself that it was make believe! I wanted to ask the rest of the cast who each of them thought was the murderer but then I reckoned they'd all probably been told at the start. It was the characters who were super nice you had to watch – I figured they were most likely to be hiding a crazy serial killer side. I felt like Sherlock Holmes walking around, trying to find clues with my assistant Holmes (Pollyanne!).

The next scene they were filming was in the visitors' centre of the donkey sanctuary. The production team had asked us to send them adoption booklets and leaflets a while back but after sending them I hadn't thought any more about it, and I could see now that they'd used them to create their own versions. They'd gone to a lot of trouble – picking up a leaflet you would think Judd Wood was a bona fide sanctuary and not one made up for a TV series. They had a big display board with blown-up photos of our donkeys on it. They'd used different names but of course I knew who was who.

On the tables were the memorabilia we have for sale when people visit the sanctuary: special cups with our donkeys' photos on the side, teapots, plates, donkey soft toys, rubbers ... little things that children can buy with their pocket money.

I had been hoping that one of the characters would end up being killed at the sanctuary but that didn't happen. It sounds morbid, but I'd wanted to see how an actor pretends to be dead! The actress who played the vet said her character ends up being dismembered and left in a hamper basket at the railway station. It was funny to be talking about it as if we were discussing the price of a pint of milk! I still didn't know who the murderer was because none of the cast would tell me – they said I had to wait and see when the episode aired. I knew it couldn't be the donkey sanctuary staff, though, because if it had been them then they would have used

Pollyanne and the rest of the donkeys in further scenes. I'll make a detective yet!

We had a long wait until we saw the episode on TV – it wasn't shown until six months had passed, which was rather frustrating because we had wanted to see it straight away. It was like having to wait for Christmas when you're a kid – it took for ever! The night it was on we all watched it in the visitors' centre on the big telly, which was quite a step up from being cramped in my tiny living room for the *Pagliacci* recording. We had the lights out so it was pretty spooky, and we all jumped out of our seats a few times when we sensed that the murderer was about to get their next victim. It was really weird seeing the people we had spent time with 'dead'.

We all tried to guess who the murderer was but we all got it wrong. I won't tell you who it is in case you ever see the episode ... I'll just say that it's not who you think!

After the credits rolled we all talked about how well the donkeys did. Stuart said he wished they'd got more air time and we all nodded. We didn't care much for the murder plot, we just wanted to see more of Pollyanne, Tracy, Charlie, Jack and the others! I didn't know it then but 5.47 million people watched the episode that night – quite astounding. If only they'd called the sanctuary Island Farm, we'd no doubt have got more visitors from it but I suppose you can't have everything. At the least the local papers would be running a story on it.

In the coming months the episode would also be appearing on TVs right across the world in over twenty-five different countries – from Australia to Russia, the United States to South Korea. I was so pleased when I found out it was going to be shown in Norway, it felt extra special because we hadn't been allowed to travel there. I was thrilled that Pollyanne was now an international star!

12

Creature Comforts

There's nothing quite like having your first ice cream of the year on a gloriously hot day. It'd been a long and cold winter, spring had been a washout but June looked like it was going to be a cracker. I was perched up on an incline, looking down at the thousands of people enjoying the last day of the Royal Bath and West Show. It was so hot the ice cream had started to melt, the strawberry sauce dripping down my wrist. I went to lick it but before I could I got pushed from behind –

Barron wanted to know when he was going to get *his* ice cream.

Linda laughed out loud and said it served me right for being so slow to eat it. I was just savouring it, I told her. I couldn't wolf down proper homemade dairy ice cream.

We'd perched ourselves up here because there were a few trees that the donkeys could use for shade, but Barron kept creeping forward because he was too inquisitive. I'd brought him here along with Diane, Bruno and Countess to do some showing and all four of them had picked up rosettes in their classes, so I was more than pleased.

We'd be going home soon but I just wanted to soak up a bit more of the atmosphere. The Royal Bath and West Show is the biggest agricultural show in the country and it takes place every May–June. I go every year but there always seems to be something new to see and do – you just can't beat it. Over a quarter of a million people attend the show over the four days it runs, but we usually come just on the last day; the best day in my opinion. There are horses, cattle, pigs, sheep, alpacas, goats, donkeys, poultry, rabbits and many more animals and birds to see. There are also food and drink competitions, a 4 × 4 driving show, floral displays, falconry, canoeing and much more. The Royal Bath and West Show is certainly somewhere you could never get bored . . . unless your name is Barron. He was looking at me with eyes that said, 'Can we go home now?'

I let him have the last bit of cone from my ice cream then walked up with him to the others. I took Barron and Bruno's lead ropes while Linda grabbed Diana and Countess. We decided to split up in the sea of cars and vans to try and find our lorry as quickly as we could. After a few minutes of searching I looked up and saw Linda frantically waved at me. She'd found it.

'Excuse me!' A voice boomed from behind me. For a moment I thought one of the donkeys had knocked someone's wing-mirror or something, but when I turned around I realised the guy wasn't angry with us – he was smiling from ear to ear. The second thing I noticed was that he was wearing a smart blue suit, he must have been boiling! He introduced himself as Martin and asked if I'd mind if he interviewed me, and I noticed for the first time that he was carrying recording equipment. He must be a journalist, I thought, and I asked which newspaper he wrote for.

It turned out that Martin wasn't a journalist at all. He worked for Aardman Animations and he told me that they might be interested in using my voice for a *Creature Comforts* voiceover. I admit I didn't really know what he was going on about, but when he said that they were the people who'd made *Wallace and Gromit*, I knew it must be a big deal.

It felt weird to be standing next to the lorry in a car park, being recorded like this. Martin told me to try to forget about the recorder, then started asking me general things about the donkeys. I was a bit nervous at first but after a minute or two I warmed up and it was fine. I talked to him like I talk to visitors at the sanctuary. Linda was up next – she hadn't been sure whether she wanted to do it, but I told her she'd be kicking herself all the way home if she didn't. After we'd both talked for a few minutes, Martin said he had enough for the time being and asked for our contact details. He thanked us one more time, before disappearing down one of the paths leading back to the showground.

'Fancy that!' I said to Linda when he was out of earshot. Out of the many thousands of people who had been at the show today, Martin had chosen to interview us. I felt very lucky to have been picked – even if our recordings were never used I wouldn't mind. I was just a bit gutted Pollyanne wasn't with us because I'd like to have told Martin her story. If he did get in touch with us again, I would have to make sure I mentioned the UK's only donkey opera star.

Martin did ring, a few weeks later. He said the people back at Aardman Animations had loved what we'd said, especially our strong Oxfordshire accents, so they wanted to record more of us, but this time at the sanctuary. They wanted to meet the donkeys and get a proper feel for the place.

We were all thrilled. We'd had lots of exciting experiences over the last year or so with Pollyanne and our other donkeys, but I must admit that we all thought it would be nice for us to take centre stage for once! *Creature Comforts* is famous for taking the voices of normal people, talking about normal things, and matching them to Plasticine animals. The resulting situations are always very funny.

When the Aardman gang arrived, they explained that everything was unscripted and everything had to be done in one take – if I said something wrong that was fine. They weren't after perfect answers to their questions. It was hard, though, I really wished they would tell me what they wanted me to say because I didn't want to disappoint them. In the end, I spoke about how intelligent donkeys are and what great characters they have – and once I got started on that they had trouble shutting me up. They also explained that it was a very long process – it could take months before our voices were matched with an animal. Sometimes you listen to a person's voice and know immediately what sort of animal they should be, they said, but sometimes it can take longer. And then actually modelling the animals from Plasticine and doing all the filming takes even longer – they have to move the model in tiny fractions to make it look as if it is talking.

Linda ended up being a donkey – and I must admit I was slightly jealous. I like to think she's Pollyanne, as the men from Aardman spent quite a while with her during their visit. They used my voice for a little white dog, sitting by the donkey pens. It was very strange to hear my voice coming out of a Plasticine dog!

Our parts were only a few seconds long, although I ended up being in three other episodes. There were only nine episodes in the series so I had quite a big part, I suppose. Everyone was buzzing about it for weeks after it was shown on TV. I joked that people would be asking for my autograph next but that I'd have to persuade one of my dogs to let me use their foot as a paw double!

13

Strike a Pose

We made so many improvements to the sanctuary over the years, but one that I'm particularly proud of is the renovation of our big barn. It's a vast space and we weren't really using it for anything – just storing junk and occasional riding lessons. With a whole team of volunteers to help us, we cleared everything out, repainted, laid down carpet and installed a kitchen. Now we can use the barn for all manner of events and it provides a nice little bit of extra income.

Today we were hosting a jumble sale and inside

the barn was a hive of activity as we got everything set up. It was due to start in an hour's time so there were lots of people frantically filling tables with an assortment of things. There were stalls selling clothes, DVDs, toys, plants and homemade treats. Our three trustees were watching over everything and helping people set up.

We couldn't function as a charity without our trustees – they help us so much and always making sure things are done properly. Running a charity is complicated stuff, so they help take some of the weight off my shoulders. I gave them a quick wave as I walked with Linda over to the book stall. She tipped the pile of Jackie Collins she was carrying onto the table for one of our volunteers to sort.

'I wonder if we'll get as many people as last time?' she asked me.

I shrugged; we could only hope so. Nearly two hundred people had come to our first sale and we'd managed to raise £900 for the sanctuary. I'd been in charge of the cooking: serving up bacon and sausage sandwiches, chips and burgers to anyone who was feeling a bit peckish. I was due to be doing the same today, with Linda taking the orders.

As we surveyed the busy scene, I decided the time was right to ask Linda a favour. Pollyanne had a big, A-list job the next day but something had come up and it looked like I wouldn't be able to go with her.

'You know the photoshoot tomorrow? Well, Harry Oliver from up near Sheffield has been on the phone and he's got a donkey with a bad leg that someone tied to his gate last night. He needs me to go and pick it up first thing . . .'

She didn't wait for me to finish. 'Okay,' she said. 'I'll do it. But you owe me!'

Linda and Pollyanne's Big Day Out

When John asked me to accompany Pollyanne to the photo-shoot, part of me wanted to say no. I am usually the one left behind with the donkeys and that's the way I like it. Why couldn't he ask Gaggy instead? But then I remembered how John was always buzzing when he came back from one of Pollyanne's showbiz adventures and I thought maybe it was about time I got a turn.

Kay met me at the sanctuary just before nine, as we didn't have to be at the shoot until 12.30. I'd spent twenty minutes before I set off trying to decide what to wear, which would have made the others laugh if they'd have known. This wasn't just any photoshoot Pollyanne was going to. This was Vogue magazine! I didn't want to look scruffy and let Pollyanne down, but at the same time I knew that even if I picked my favourite outfit, it still wouldn't have been 'in fashion'. In the end I chose my smartest pair of work jeans, boots and a maroon polo shirt with the Island Farm logo on it.

The shoot was taking place in the Big Sky Studios in central London. It just looked like a normal building – nothing especially glamorous. As soon as I opened the main door to the studio I realised the shoot was going to be nothing like I had imagined. I thought it would be super sophisticated, with super-slim models floating around in dresses and heels, sipping champagne. I'd never actually seen inside a copy of Vogue, just the odd cover on the magazine rack, but I knew it was all about fashion and luxury. I was absolutely gobsmacked by the scene in front of me and stood rooted to the spot until someone came and shouted, 'And this must be Pollyanne!' Before I could reply, he was already moving away in the direction of a man wearing a Union Jack suit with a huge painted top hat. 'Just go in that corner till we need you!' he shouted, not turning round.

The room was filled with an crazy assortment of people, animals and props. The theme of the shoot was apparently 'Merrie England' and the scene looked to me like something out of Alice in Wonderland. There was a bearded man with his face painted red, wearing a jacket made from rags and bells; a man with a huge floral decoration covering his whole body so all you could see was his legs; three people dressed all in black with soot-covered faces carrying sticks and a drum; two teenagers dressed in traditional farming clothing stood near by with tools. I found out later that they

224

weren't models at all, but the youngest dry-stone wallers in the UK.

I didn't fully understand what Pollyanne's role was to be until a model wearing the weirdest costume in the room walked towards me. She was wearing a jumpsuit made from sacking, with patches on the knees, and a strange red and black wooden mask that covered everything apart from her eyes. Her mouth was hidden so I could barely understand a word she was saying. She was going to be riding Pollyanne in the photos, but facing backwards. Very strange! I didn't understand what this was supposed to symbolise but I was just glad there was hardly any flesh on the model ... if she'd been a more normal size I'd have had to refuse.

When it was our turn to be photographed, I led Pollyanne onto the set and made sure she was standing exactly where the photographer wanted her. I helped the model up and one of the assistants placed a wooden necklace around the model's neck and a necklace of wild flowers around Pollyanne's neck. The photographer for the shoot was called Tim Walker and he moved around Pollyanne, taking photographs from every angle. I didn't know until later that Tim is a big deal in the fashion world, to me he just seemed a down-to-earth kind of fella. He has photographed lots of important fashion icons, like Vivienne Westwood, Alexander McQueen, Madonna and Lily Cole. Who would have thought that our Pollyanne would have something in common with Madonna!

It took about ten minutes for Tim to get the photos he wanted and then the assistant moved us to one side and the model dismounted. We were told we could go home so after waving a quick goodbye to the other models we headed for the exit.

I was so excited the day the July edition of Vogue came into the shops that I couldn't stop smiling – the girl behind the checkout at Sainsbury's must have wondered what was going on, as I'm not the sort of person who buys Vogue with my weekly shop. I couldn't wait to rip open the plastic film and see Pollyanne looking up at me. I raced back to the sanctuary and started flicking through the pages, searching for her. Finally, on page 106, there she was. The picture they had chosen showed Pollyanne mid hee-haw, which maybe wasn't *her best angle! I didn't mind, though. What an achievement! Pollyanne was officially a* Vogue *model.*

If I thought the Vogue *shoot was strange, then nothing could prepare me for my next experience with Pollyanne. For this job, Pollyanne would be appearing in a whole scene of the TV show* Not Going Out, *and John asked me whether I'd mind going along in his place again as he had a few things he needed to do at the sanctuary.*

Not Going Out *is filmed in front of a live studio audience at Pinewood Studios in Teddington. It was a lovely summer's day and people were wearing an assortment of summer dresses, shorts and flip-flops, but as I pulled up to the studio I saw a huge queue of people outside . . . wearing Santa hats and tinsel. I was starting to realise that when it came to show-business, anything goes, but it still struck me as rather odd. It was only later that I realised the episode we were taking part in was the Christmas special and the people outside were queuing to be in the audience.*

Kay had been to Pinewood Studios plenty of times and

explained that all sorts of famous movies had been filmed there, including Mamma Mia!, The Dark Knight, Pirates of the Caribbean . . . she just kept listing big movie after big movie. It made me feel a bit nervous to be honest – I started to wonder if I'd bump into Johnny Depp or Christian Bale in the corridor!

The actors were very nice and all came over to give Pollyanne a stroke before the cameras started rolling. The comedian Lee Mack plays the main part; he was wandering around wearing a dressing gown, looking very relaxed and chatting to everyone. When it came time for him to film the scene, he took the dressing gown off and I got the shock of my life. He was naked! I didn't know where to look, I can tell you. He had his back to me to begin with and when he turned round I realised he actually had something preserving his modesty, which was a bit of a relief.

For some reason the scene involved Lee hanging upside down, 'naked', with an orange in his mouth. They told me it was a dream sequence, which I suppose explained a lot. All Pollyanne had to do was stand in front of him, but I had to lie on the floor with my arm ready to grab Pollyanne if needed. I concentrated on looking at Pollyanne and ignored the scantily clad Lee! Thankfully it all went well on the first take so the director said there was no need to do it again.

We got out of there as quickly as possible and Kay and I laughed all the way home. I had been so embarrassed, but of course Pollyanne hadn't been bothered in the slightest!

14

Encore!

It was an awful day. Rain, wind, and set for thunder and lightning. The chickens had wisely decided to stay in the coop and the donkeys were getting a bit restless in their stables. Unlike them, I would have loved to stay indoors. But no such luck. There were jobs to be done. I just had to pull on my waterproofs and wellies and get on with them. The sanctuary was officially open, as always, but thankfully there were no visitors to attend to on top of everything else. My priority today was the roof of the office. It was leaking, so I had to do my best to fix it as soon as possible. I climbed a ladder to the roof, thinking to myself that the office really was on its last legs. I found the source of the leak and set about fixing it up. This office would have to last a bit longer yet. Donations were down and unless we could raise more money soon, the future was looking bleak.

I was on my way back down the ladder when Stuart came tearing out of the office and nearly knocked me off. He apologised but explained that he was in a rush – Kay was on the phone! I couldn't wait to speak to her. Maybe she had a little job for Pollyanne. I hoped so – that could help us pay the latest vet's bill which was now several weeks overdue. I stepped inside, water was pouring off me and forming a puddle around my feet. Wendy handed me the phone. Kay and I hadn't talked for a few months and I'd been worried that work for donkeys had dried up. Kay reassured me it hadn't. In fact, she said, some old friends had been in touch about Pollyanne's availability … I was confused, but then I twigged: we would be returning to the Royal Opera House.

Pollyanne would be performing in the opera *Carmen*, but this time the team at the Royal Opera House needed *me* to be in it too! My heart sank. I went from feeling on top of the world to the pits of despair. There was no way I could do it, no way at all. I had been stricken by stage fright just rehearsing with Pollyanne last time. The thought of having to act in front of two thousand people was too horrible. I would have to tell her no.

But for some reason when I opened my mouth, what came out instead was, 'Yes'.

'That's great,' said Kay. 'First rehearsal is next Monday, so I'll see you at 7.30 a.m.'

Stuart appeared behind me, and gave me a strange look. 'Are you okay, Dad?'

I just stood there with my mouth wide open, not saying a word.

A few moments passed before I explained that I'd just agreed to appear alongside Pollyanne in an opera.

Wendy immediately snatched the phone out of my hand before I could ring Kay back and tell her I'd changed my mind. I felt sick to the stomach, but I knew deep down I had to do it. We badly needed the money and it was well-paid work for a few months. Pollyanne would love it, too. I had sensed that she missed being in the limelight, and it would be nice to catch up with our friends.

The first rehearsal day soon arrived, and on the way down to London with Kay I had a strong feeling of déjà vu. She talked me through the plot of *Carmen* and the different opera singers who would playing the lead roles.

Carmen is a passionate love story, set in Seville, Spain. The lead character is a beautiful gypsy seductress named Carmen. She begins a relationship with a soldier, Don José, who ends up giving up everything – his former lover, his career – to be with her. But Don José is a jealous man, and when Carmen starts a relationship with a bullfighter called Escamillo, he kills her. It seemed to me that *all* operas are about jealousy and murder.

Anna Caterina Antonacci was to play Carmen, Jonas Kaufmann was to play Don José, and Ildebrando D'Arcangelo was to play Escamillo. I asked Kay to write their names down on a piece of paper for me – it wouldn't be the end of the world if I forgot them but I wanted to try and get them right. If they took the time to remember Pollyanne's name, it was the least I could do . . . I was a bit saddened to realise that I wouldn't be seeing the cast from *Pagliacci* again, but many of the crew would be the same, and Kay assured me that they were looking forward to welcoming Pollyanne back to the stage.

Kay had said she needed four chickens to appear in the opera and so I had picked out our four best – chickens that both like being handled and that looked good. Some people would have said I was silly for spending so long choosing the right ones. A chicken is a chicken, after all. But I care about all the animals and birds we have at the sanctuary and I would never risk causing distress to any one of them. Okay, I admit I probably looked daft placing a radio beside their coop so that they could get used to loud music … but I really thought it would be beneficial as they would have a whole orchestra to contend with once they reached the Royal Opera House.

Our drive down didn't take long and we were soon getting ready for our first run-through. As I stood in the wings, I gripped Pollyanne's lead rope so tightly that my hand throbbed. Compared to Pollyanne's role in *Pagliacci*, we had a much bigger part to play in *Carmen*. We would be appearing in Acts I and III. My heart was beating fast, and I had a strong urge to make a run for it. I tried to remember what Linda had said before we left this morning. 'You're doing this for all the donkeys, the ones we have now, and the ones we'll need to save in the future.' I needed to focus. If Pollyanne could do it, so could I.

On the other side of the stage, waiting in the wings, was a big black horse who went by the name of Louis. He was making his big stage debut as Escamillo's horse. I had chatted to his owner briefly but I knew we'd be catching up properly once the first run-through was over.

On cue, we stepped onto the stage and into the lights, Pollyanne wearing some pannier baskets on either side of her, filled with old-fashioned wine flagons. We were to walk over to a group of people playing the villagers. Then I had to offer them a drink from one of the wine flagons, and they would accept. Someone leant forward and told me in broken English not to worry, I was doing fine. I didn't understand how he knew I was nervous, but then I noticed my hands were shaking like mad. I turned and stroked Pollyanne's face, which helped calm me down. The men returned the flagons, which was my signal to move on. I led Pollyanne to the other side of the stage, where another group were gathered. I was to offer them a drink too. I tried my best to laugh along as they pretended to be sharing a funny story. It was hard, and I'm sure I was as wooden as a post, but I knew it would get easier the more rehearsals we did. There was lots going on in other sections of the stage but I tried to concentrate on our part, and what we had to do next. As soon as Carmen appeared behind us, we were to turn and leave the stage.

Back in the wings, Kay took Pollyanne and put her in her pen for me. We had quite a wait until our scene in Act III, so I had time to meet Louis's owner, Samantha Jones. Samantha was so excited about Louis's big break. She had met Ildebrando D'Arcangelo a few weeks earlier, to teach him how to ride with his back straight like a matador, but today was Louis's first time at the Royal Opera House. Kay explained that Louis was a confident horse who didn't seem to let things affect him. Usually a horse would bolt if it got frightened, but Louis remained calm all the time. He wasn't at all bothered by all the singers, and didn't have a problem with Ildebrando singing while riding him. He was a smashing horse, so handsome. I gave him a mint I had in my pocket and he munched it in no time at all. He seemed smitten with Pollyanne: he kept glancing over at her and flicking his tail.

It was almost time for us to go on again. Emily came to collect us, and Pollyanne happily trotted out of her pen, looking forward to being back onstage. This time around it was not wine in the baskets but ammunition. As I loaded her up, she didn't seem bothered at all. Rather, she looked at me as if to say, 'Get a move on!' and started to creep forward, eager to step into the bright lights. When I was ready, I gave her a little tap on her rump and she was off, leading me through the crowds of people.

The stage had been transformed since Act I. Now it was dressed to look like a battleground, with small – controlled – fires burning at regular intervals. We had to weave our way in between them. I was slightly con-cerned about Pollyanne, who to my knowledge had never seen fire before – or certainly not at this proxim-ity – and I didn't know how she would react. The fires were blasting out some strong heat too. I could feel beads of sweat forming on my forehead. Pollyanne didn't even give the fires a second glance and as if she had actually read the stage directions herself, she trotted up to a group of singers playing gypsies at the front of the stage. The gypsies were supposed to be a frightening bunch but without makeup, wearing T-shirts and jeans, they didn't quite cut it. My role in this scene was as a peasant farmer trying to sell my donkey and my ammunition to one of the gypsies. The deal done, I was to hand Pollyanne over for her to be led away. Needless to say, she went with him without a backward glance.

All hell broke then loose on stage, as the action called for a gunfight. The sound effects were very realistic but Pollyanne didn't react, she just carried on, standing next to her 'new owner'. We all walked over to a canopy where we had to wait for the rest of the chorus to come in. When they did, we made our way off stage. All in all our part in Act III was about five minutes long.

Kay met us backstage. I hadn't been half as nervous as I had been earlier, so I told her it had all gone well. I was sure I'd be absolutely fine come opening night. Having Pollyanne beside me really helped because she seemed to give me confidence in myself. The wardrobe lady I'd met during *Pagliacci* came over and gave me a huge hug.

'It's lovely to see you again,' she told me. She explained that she'd left my costume folded up on my chair, just a simple shirt, trousers, jacket and hat. There was a smoking pipe too. 'I hope you don't mind,' she said, 'but we'd love it if you grew a beard. We think it would look more authentic because a working man back then wouldn't have been clean shaven.'

I told her I wouldn't mind at all. While we were there I spoke to Emily to ask whether I could bring Tracy with me next time, as well as Pollyanne, as I wanted her to learn the part in case Pollyanne fell ill. Emily thought it was a great idea.

As rehearsals continued, Pollyanne seemed to enjoy herself more and more. She seemed to know exactly when to move, so we never missed any of our stage cues. During one rehearsal the director decided he wanted us to move slightly over to the left to fill in a bit of the stage that was empty but Pollyanne wouldn't have it. She refused to budge, and after a lot of huffing and puffing I had to give up. The director didn't mind: Pollyanne didn't want to get her part wrong and was determined to do everything exactly as she had been taught.

Before I knew it, it was opening night. I had rehearsed more than twenty times and I should have been feeling totally relaxed ... but I wasn't at all. I was a gibbering wreck. My throat was so dry I could hardly speak and I'd had no more than three hours' sleep the night before. I felt even more apprehensive than I had done on the opening night of *Pagliacci*. I hadn't seen the wardrobe lady since our first rehearsal but she popped over to wish us good luck, and told me my beard was spot on.

And then we were told we'd be performing in front of royalty. My stomach started doing back-flips. Even the professionals were nervous. *Carmen* is a huge opera, and it was opening night, and so the audience was awash with reviewers and celebrities and opera buffs waiting to see if we did a good job. There was no room for error. If the reviews panned the production, the whole team would be devastated. As the lights went down, I knew it was crunch time. We would all just have to put our best foot – and hoof – forward, and do our best.

Pollyanne was amazing. She didn't care that there were two thousand people in the audience, nor did she care who they were – royalty or glitterati or regular Joe Bloggs. The second she appeared on stage, the audience clapped and cheered wildy. They weren't looking at me, but I felt ever so self-conscious all the same. I pulled the brim of my hat down so it hid part of my face and stopped me from being able to look out at the audience. Unlike Pollyanne, I knew that I'd freeze if I looked up and saw Prince Charles or one of the other members of the royal family staring down at me. The whole thing passed in a surreal dream ...

After the performance the cast had to line up for a meet and greet. So many people stopped to say hello to Pollyanne and to tell me how nice it was to see a donkey on stage. I recognised one chap but it took me a while to place him as David Dimbleby. He spent a long time talking to me and was horrified when he found out Pollyanne had been destined for slaughter. He was joined by Charles Kennedy, then leader of the Liberal Democrats, who wanted to find out more about Pollyanne and the work we did at the sanctuary. I completely lost track of time. I met celebrities, people from other opera companies who had flown in especially to see the performance, and important people from the Royal Opera House itself. At 11 p.m. I politely excused myself and Pollyanne. We had to head home. Pollyanne looked awfully disappointed to leave her adoring fans!

We didn't know it that night but Pollyanne was going be starring in *Carmen* for many more years to come. To date she has performed over six hundred times. In fact, although the cast has changed time and time again, Pollyanne and Louis the stallion have performed in every production since that first one in front of royalty.

She could do her part blindfolded now, but you never get the sense that she's bored – her tail is always swishing when she comes off stage. Even after a long break of a year or more, she remembers every little detail. If an actor accidentally stands in her place she will gently nuzzle him with her nose to move him out of the way. She catches them quite unawares sometimes!

Remarkably, she has never, ever, had an accident on stage, which the crew tell me is quite remarkable. I can generally recognise the warning signs – she raises her tail – but I give her a little tap and she lowers it back down again. She then looks at me as if to say, 'Sorry for even thinking about it.' This has only happened a couple of times and she'll just go in the corner of her pen once she's come off stage which makes it easy to clean up.

That said, there is a contingency plan, just in case – the cast have several brushes, dustpans and mops on the stage (in keeping with the period, of course!) so they can scoop up anything and get rid of it before someone steps in it or trips over. When the chickens are on stage, they occasionally lay an egg or two! I've had nightmares about tripping up on them and landing head first in the orchestra pit.

Reviewers have almost always given our production of *Carmen* rave reviews, much to the delight of the cast and crew. Many reviewers have said that the best production was the first one we did – they called it a 'revelation' – but I seem to enjoy each one more than the last. It has become a firm favourite with opera goers. We get so excited every time we get a phone call to tell us that the Royal Opera House have decided to put it on again.

I no longer get stage fright and look forward to appearing on stage with Pollyanne. I also enjoy mingling with the huge cast. Each time there are at least 150 people so it takes a while to get used to people's names. Many of the people we have met and worked with over the years have taken it upon themselves to raise money for the sanctuary by sponsoring Pollyanne and her friends. They all make a fuss of Tracy too when she comes along to rehearsals. She acts as Pollyanne's understudy, but as yet Pollyanne has never been ill or needed to miss a show. They might be the bestest of friends, but I don't think Pollyanne would like to share her place in the spotlight just yet – she loves being the official Royal Opera House donkey too much!

Afterword

Little Donkey

If Pollyanne could talk she'd probably say that Christmas Eve is her favourite day of the year. It's definitely her busiest. Linda and I find it quite stressful because we have to get all our timings right, otherwise we could disappoint a lot of people.

'Is Pollyanne going to be at church later?' a little boy asked me as I handed his mum a laminated donkey card.

'She sure is, she'll be there at three o'clock,' I told him. 'Why don't you go and see if you can find her now, she's over in that paddock.'

Without saying anything more he ran off, his mum following ten steps behind. 'Christopher! What have I told you about running off!' she called but it was no use, he was on a mission to find Pollyanne. The donkey cards had been Wendy's idea and were a big hit with visitors and volunteers. On each laminated card are little photos of the ten donkeys you can adopt and next to each photo is a colour, which matches the donkey's collar. Each collar is just a loop made out of woven material and it hangs over their necks, so it doesn't cause them any discomfort or anything. It makes things a whole lot simpler because visitors can easily spot the donkey they've sponsored without having to find me, Linda or Gaggy to point them out. In the old days we'd try to point out Pollyanne in the middle of ten or so other don-keys and it'd be like *Mission Impossible*. She's the donkey four back and three to the left! Then one of the donkeys would move and we'd have to start all over again. It also makes a fun game for the children who visit because they like to try to find every donkey on the card.

We'd opened the barn for the day, and were serving mince pies and refreshments inside. Families were sitting around at the tables in the barn, drinking mulled wine. I walked over to some tables we'd put out to sell some of our memorabilia and the official Island Farm Donkey Sanctuary Christmas cards – designed and painted by one of our supporters. Half of the things had already been sold and there was only one pack of cards left.

Before I knew it, it was two o'clock – time for us to get Pollyanne ready for her church performance. Linda came out of the kitchen, leaving a volunteer to hold the fort until we officially closed at four o'clock. As soon as I went to the paddock gate Pollyanne trotted over, she knew it was show time.

'Hello again,' I said to the flustered mum as she tried to find some seats for herself and young Christopher, who seemed to have quietened down since we spoke at the sanctuary. 'I think there's a couple on the third row.'

The church was absolutely packed: it seemed every man, woman and child from Wantage had turned up to the church's Christmas Eve mass. I was going to be sitting at the front with Linda and Pollyanne, but first Pollyanne had to perform the nativity story with the children from the Sunday School. Pollyanne loves children and the children at the church love her too; the priest had insisted that Pollyanne was the donkey I brought because they see her as *their* donkey. The church had been decorated with hundreds of candles – in all the alcoves, on all the window ledges, on the altar. Even though it was only three o'clock the sky had already started to turn dark. It looked really magical.

The priest started the service with a prayer and then the children took to the stage. One of the Sunday School teachers helped to lift the little girl playing Mary onto Pollyanne's back and then down again when they reached the stable. Once they'd finished, the young boy who had been playing Joseph brought Pollyanne over, so she could stand next to me until the service finished.

It was during the third carol that Pollyanne, the veteran stage performer, let one off. I was hoping that no one had heard, but no such luck. It was really loud and the children sitting near me all started giggling. As the priest started to give his message she did it again, and again. She wasn't at all bothered and was shaking her tail from side to side as if she was fanning it out to make sure that as many people as possible smelt it! Half the congregation seemed to be trying their best to stifle their giggles. In the end the priest even made a joke about her wind problem, saying she was going to blow all the candles out. She certainly made the service unforgettable.

As soon as the service finished Linda and I jumped up and I grabbed Pollyanne's lead rope to lead her out as quickly as possible. To some people this would seem a bit unfriendly, but we've learnt by experience that if we stay seated we get swamped. Everyone wants to see Pollyanne and stroke her but there simply isn't enough time – it would take hours. We had another service to get to in Oxford so there was no way we could stay long at all.

By the time the Oxford church service had finished my voice was hoarse. I'd lost count of the number of times I'd sung *Away in a Manger* and *O Come All Ye Faithful* over the last two weeks. Pollyanne had been as good as gold and although she shook her tail a few times she hadn't repeated her earlier performance, thank goodness! We'd heard Pollyanne's favourite Christmas carol *Little Donkey* at every event we'd been to during the Christmas season – it is the loudest song because the children give it extra oomph. They sing it specially for Pollyanne, thinking that she is the donkey that Mary rode to Bethlehem.

After dropping Linda off at her mum's in the village I drove the lorry back to the sanctuary. There was no sign of anyone on the roads – it seemed like everyone apart from Pollyanne and myself were tucked up waiting for Father Christmas to deliver their presents. The security light switched on as we pulled up into the car park and

I could see Corky, Patch, Tubby and Candy were pressing themselves up against the gate, jumping up and barking.

'Quieten down, lads. I'll be just one minute,' I called to them as I went to lower the ramp to let Pollyanne out. Tubby ran around in a circle in excitement. 'Come on, girl, we're home now.' I spoke into the darkness of the lorry. Pollyanne stepped forward and nuzzled her head into my chest. I stroked her face and gave her a kiss on the top of her head. 'Tracy will be wondering where you are!' I told her.

We walked slowly over to the gate, both of us tired from the day's activities. The second I opened the gate the dogs were jumping up, weaving between my legs. I grabbed a tennis ball from the ground and chucked it in the direction of the yard. All four of them ran off to get it and I knew they'd be tumbling and play fighting for the next few minutes at least. Pollyanne was still by my side, she's more than used to the dogs' crazy behaviour. I rested my arm on her back and together we made our way to the girls' shelter. I felt something cold land on my face, looked up and saw the first snowflakes beginning to fall – it looked as if we were going to have a white Christmas.

Pollyanne looked up at the snowflakes too, then back at me. She was so happy, she'd really enjoyed being made a fuss of at the two churches. She leant into me again so I would stroke her some more before she had to make her way inside with the others. The girls were all under the roof, keeping warm, but the second they saw me and Pollyanne they rushed over, pushing each other out of the way. They were pressing so much against the gate that I struggled to open it. 'Out of the way, Diana. You too, Tracy. Let me in!' I tried to appear angry, but they all knew I was messing about. Eventually they moved back so I could open the gate wide enough to let us through. The snow was still falling so I made my way underneath the shelter so they didn't get soaked by it – I didn't want any of them to end up catching a cold. I tried my best to stroke as many as I could but I was completely surrounded, all of the girls pestering me for a cuddle. I stayed there for a while, looking out as the snow fell, blanketing everything. After ten minutes everything was covered in several inches of snow, but I was bone dry under the shelter. The donkeys started to wander off but Pollyanne and Tracy stayed with me, just enjoying being by my side. The snow made everything look clean and beautiful; it was so peaceful. I couldn't have been any happier. The silence didn't last long, the dogs soon appeared on the other side of the gate, barking to let me know that they had the ball and wanted me to throw it for them again. It rolled underneath the gate so I took it and threw it in the direction of the old office. We wouldn't be using the office in the New Year – we'd received another portable classroom a few weeks earlier and it had been thoroughly cleaned and painted. I'd be helping Stuart move everything over in the next week or so. Things were looking up again, we had fantastic shelters for the donkeys, a visitors' centre, fully equipped barn and now a new office ... and we'd just received the news that Pollyanne would be starring in *Carmen* again at the Royal Opera House in the spring.

'See you tomorrow, girls,' I said as I gave Pollyanne and Tracy one last cuddle. 'Watch out Father Christmas and his reindeers don't pinch your carrots!'

Acknowledgements

First of all I'd like to thank my fantastic editor, Hannah Boursnell, and everyone at Little, Brown for making me feel so welcome. Hannah provided so much encouragement and support during the writing process, I will be forever grateful. I would also like to thank my lovely agent Araminta Whitley at Lucas Alexander Whitley for her guidance and enthusiasm.

I want to say a huge thank you to John McLaren, Judy Gibbons, Stuart McLaren, Linda, Wendy and Gaggy at Island Farm Donkey Sanctuary for being so welcoming and accommodating during my time with them – they are truly amazing and I have never met more selfless people. The work they do for the donkeys is astounding and I know I have made friends for life. I also want to thank Kay Weston at Animal Ambassadors and Emily Gottlieb, Stage Manager at the Royal Opera House, for their input.

Thank you to everyone who helped with this book: Sophie Hughes, Beryl Benson, Lynne Greason, Elaine Henderson, Joanne Brooks, Wendy Hindley and Rosie Parker. I'd also like to thank the animals in my life, my cats Tobey, Sooty and Teddy and my dogs Chev, Dave and Pete. I am animal-mad, so being able to write this book was a dream come true.

Above all, I'd like to thank all the donkeys at Island Farm (sadly I don't have room to list you all!), Tracy, Barron, Loppy, Jack, Charli . . . and of course Pollyanne!

And finally, thank you to Professor Gill Davies, opera fan and publishing legend, who met Pollyanne backstage at the Royal Opera House and started this whole thing in motion.

Visit Island Farm!

Island Farm
Donkey Sanctuary
near Wallingford
donkeyrescue.co.uk

If you enjoyed reading about Pollyanne and her friends,
why not pay them a visit at Island Farm Donkey Sanctuary?

Island Farm Donkey Sanctuary
Old Didcot Road,
Brightwell-Cum-Sotwell,
Wallingford,
Oxfordshire
OX10 0SW

Tel: 01491 833938

Open daily from 11 a.m. to 4 p.m., except Christmas Day.
Admission Free.

For more information or to make a donation, visit
www.donkeyrescue.co.uk.

Adopt a Donkey!

If you would like to adopt Pollyanne or another Island Farm
donkey, either for yourself or as a gift, please visit our website
at www.donkeyrescue.co.uk. For £15 per year, you'll receive a
beautiful photograph of your donkey, plus an adoption
certificate and details about his or her life story. The money
helps us to feed and look after the donkeys and ensures we
are able to continue rescuing other animals in need.